THE JOURNEY BACK TO ME

SHE SAID YES TO UNCOVERING THE TREASURE WITHIN ...

CHRISTEL MORGAN WEST

The Journey Back to Me: She Said Yes to Uncovering the Treasures
Within

Copyright © 2018 by Christel Morgan West

For Author inquiries please contact:

Contact the Author via email: Christelwest11@gmail.com

Website: www.christelwest.com

For Publishers inquiries please contact:

ISpeak Publishing Services

http://www.ispeakpublishing.com

Contact the Publisher via email: ISpeakPublish@gmail.com

All Scriptures come from the King James Version (KJV), New International Version (NIV)

New Living Translation (NLT) of the Holy Bible unless otherwise indicated.

Disclaimer

All the material contained in this book is provided for educational and informational purposes only. No responsibility can be taken for any results or outcomes resulting from the use of this material.

While every attempt has been made to provide information that is both accurate and effective, the author does not assume any responsibility for the accuracy or use/misuse of this information.

Printed in the United States of America

ISBN 978-0-692-15888-3

ISpeak Publishing Service

Little Rock, AR.

501-519-6996

Forewords

Maybe you are where I once was in life — stuck. I had accepted Christ as my Savior. But instead of walking in the true anointing of the power of the Holy Spirit, I continued to live in bondage. I had bought into the lie that I could get past my problems on my own.

My afflictions continued to haunt me, and unforeseen circumstances continuously imprisoned me and my family. The normal rituals of going to church, reading Scripture and surrounding myself with like-minded people only carried me halfway. (We like-minded people all swam in a pool of religion instead of conquering through the power of the anointing of Jesus Christ. Our prayers all sounded alike, our dress mimicked that of our church-mates and, sadly, judgment reigned in all directions.) I was caught up in religion, not faith; tradition, not power. I was sick, I was tired, and I was struggling financially. Even worse, I believed all this was the will of God.

Finally, I cried out to Him: "*Please* give me an extra measure of faith! Bring into my life people who will love me and invest in me. Show me who I am in You! Heal my body! Make me whole!"

And eight years ago, God brought Christel West into my life. She was that answered prayer. We had a divine connection that was extremely powerful. Together we prayed, we cried, and we overcame. She poured into my thirsty spirit, showing me who I was in Christ: highly favored, anointed, divinely appointed and more than a conqueror. Christ, through Christel, cast out my old way of thinking and poured in a powerful, anointed new way. "Who told you God wanted you to be sick?" she asked me. "That is not right. Through the stripes of Jesus, you are healed! Walk in it. Who told you that you had to dress like that? You are a Queen! Queens look beautiful. Queen Esther dressed beautifully. And eye has not seen, nor ear heard, all that the Lord has for YOU!"

I learned that I had all authority through Christ Jesus to take my life back. And I began walking in spirit, not flesh. Through the many lessons Christel poured into me, I was given an extra measure of faith. Today, I am living the life of one favored, divinely anointed, and chosen by the Creator of the Universe. No weapon formed against me shall prosper. If God is for me, who is against me? His Word will not return void. Yes, I AM bold and courageous. I AM full of an extra measure of faith. I AM clothed in His righteousness. I AM exceedingly blessed. I welcome you into your journey of finding God's power inside you. May the old be cast away and may His transforming power bring you into the new. God bless your journey!

Thank You, Jesus, for the anointing upon us all. Thank You for using my dear friend, Christel West, to pour Your light into me. I pray that every person reading this book will be transformed into powerful vessels for Your glory.

Keep Shining,

Kristin Druey

My life experience was similar to that of my daughter, Christel. I was molested at the age of 5 and didn't speak of it for years, but the effects of the experience were far-reaching. I was stuck. I stayed depressed. I didn't love myself. I didn't think I deserved anything good; even when I received a gift I really liked, I'd tell myself that I should give it away. Not knowing the real Wanda, I was existing rather than living. We have eyes to see physically, but sometimes we don't see with our spiritual or mental eyes because of our mindset. Unfortunately, my daughter suffered from my lack of self-love.

I thank GOD for opening my spiritual eyes and awakening me to my knowledge of the real me. Just as He has forgiven me my sins, I have forgiven myself ... not only for the things I did, but also the things I didn't do. I can now say I love, and like, *me*. I walk in complete freedom.

And, praise GOD, my daughter has forgiven me. We are closer now than we've ever been, and I am her biggest cheerleader.

In these pages, Christel shares frankly about her childhood, which was marred by the generational curse I passed down to her. I don't take this personally; ours is a story full of lessons to help others. Christel did her soulwork in order to be set free of the bondage in which she'd struggled. GOD used her to help me do the same. Now that I have learned to use my voice, I can say I'm living as my True Self!

Wanda Price

Dedication

I dedicate this book to my family. Without you in my life, I would not have been able to stand face-front and be the woman I am today.

To my husband, Marco West, who has stood with me through every layer that was uncovered: You saw something in me that I did not see in myself. Through your dedication, commitment and unwavering love, I was able to uncover the things I chose to hide. While my journey to finding me was painful, your love — GOD's love through you — anchored me and caused me to persevere through it all.

To my children, grandchildren, and generations to come: This journey was most important because of each of you. I lived a life full of lies and fear, and if I was going to truly leave a legacy, it needed to be one of love and freedom. Each of you has inspired and motivated me in your own unique way, which is why I never gave up. As you take your personal journeys, remember that no matter what *anyone* thinks about you, it's what you believe about yourself that is most important. It was love that lifted and delivered me (GOD's love and self-love) and it will also sustain you ... my seeds.

To my mother: Your unwavering love, support, and sacrifices have sustained me in so many ways. Your love walk has been the greatest example a daughter could ask for. Thank you for believing and receiving the GOD in me. Thank you for being what you needed to be for my children and me so that we could fulfill our purpose.

Acknowledgments

I would like to thank my publisher, Tiffany Moorer of ISpeak Publishing, for being an awesome leader and mentor. It was through her mentoring program, our conversations, her compassion, and her heart to see me succeed that I was inspired to keep pushing to deliver my story. I would also like to thank my editor, Helaine R. Williams of Make it Plain Ministries, who came alongside Tiffany to listen, share, encourage, and inspire me through her writing gifts. She assured me that no matter what weapons tried to form against the birth of this book, we were not aborting … we were going to make it happen. It's because of these divine connections that you are reading this. I will forever be grateful for these two women, for without them, my story would still reside within me. Thank you both for helping me PUSH.

In addition, I would like to thank my stepmom, Phyllis Bah, for covering me daily, praying for me even when I couldn't pray for myself.

Lastly, I want to thank everyone who has been a part of my journey; who has stuck in there with me through my unveiling. I appreciate each of you. To all those who loved me to this place, whose love remained consistent, I am eternally grateful for you. It was love that lifted, healed and delivered me through each of you. LOVE WINS!

Table of Contents

Introduction 1

Chapter One: The Journey Begins 3

Chapter Two: I Can't CHANGE What I'm Not Willing to CONFRONT 11

Chapter Three: Wanting to be Heard, but Having Lost My Voice: 20

Chapter Four: Unconscious Seeds (Twins) 34

Chapter Five: Archetype to My Survival: The Orphans of My Soul 45

Chapter Six: I Choose ME 62

Chapter Seven: Delivered ... AND Set Free 75

Chapter Eight: A Degree of Success 90

Chapter Nine: She Said Yes! 105

A Final Word 120

Bibliography 122

About Christel West 124

Introduction

As a young teenager and single mother, I looked for love in all the wrong places. I lost my identity by covering it up due to fear and shame. When I realized that covering it up was keeping my pain in, I made a conscious decision to be naked and not ashamed. I would become transparent for all to see. In order for me to be liberated from my fears, it was a must that I face them.

I once thought my past defined me, but now I understand that this was all part of my history. We must revisit history for answers to our present circumstances, much like how we learn in history class in school. As people, we were taught history at an early age. But it was not OUR history — who we are, where we come from, why we are the way we are. Even the history lessons we *did* receive were quite vague. But then, all history is open for discussion.

There is so much I wanted to know about myself. (If I do not study history and learn for myself, who am I to teach?) Therefore, I willingly took the journey ... the one that, for you and me, is not so favorable. I faced my fears one by one, each time liberating myself from the invisible chains I created within my mind —

chains that held me captive. I had to find a way to break free. Freedom is a choice, and I made the choice to not only be free, but also share my journey to help others do the same.

My life journey, and the struggles I have seen, have inspired me to remain naked and not ashamed. This is the only way I will be able to find my True Self, uncover the treasure within, and lead you to do the same.

Chapter One
The Journey Begins

We are now going to set the stage for the story that will be told. Sit back and grab yourself a strong cup of coffee, because you will not want to put this one down.

It's 2013. I am leaving my adopted home in the Conway, Arkansas area to travel back to my original home of Detroit, Michigan, and go on trial for identity theft. I am being accused of stealing someone else's identity, when in reality, it was my *identity that was stolen. I have worked very hard to prepare for this moment. I am finally in a happy place in my life, and I feel confident that I can walk into this courtroom and face my accusers ... every one of them. I am so sick and tired of hiding behind a mask of guilt and shame, believing all the lies I had been told about my life and who I am. To think that I accepted these lies for so many years! Now it's time to take the stand. I know it won't be easy, but it must be done. I'm just a little nervous, but I know GOD is with me.*

I've got my bags packed for the trip. My flight leaves at 8 a.m. I feel so much better now that I am finally getting this behind me.

My earthly king, my husband Marco, is by my side. He and GOD, my heavenly King, are my anchors. They have kept me steady while I liberate my True Self.

As I watch this man scurry around, getting his last-minute things together before we walk out into the early-morning darkness, my mind starts drifting to how my True Self began to emerge. It's like I'm going into the birthing room, knowing that the labor will be intense ... knowing that every time I step into that courtroom, I will be fighting hard to be free. Despite that thought, I am at peace. All I can think of is my biggest fan and motivator – Marco. He is a reflection of how strong I truly am.

I can't even begin to describe the joy I felt in my heart when we reconnected. My relationship with my husband had begun in 1989 when we were kids; even then, we knew we had something special. We'd gone our separate ways after I became pregnant, and we'd reconnected in 2013. That was when I'd found my voice. GOD had placed him back into my life. And through him, GOD told me I couldn't stay quiet anymore; that I had to share my story about my journey back to me. I needed some convincing, but Marco was relentless. He is such a smooth-talking brother ... so direct and to the point. Because of him, there was an awakening in me. He was my detoxifier, flushing the silence out and releasing the truth within me. He challenged me every step of the way, forcing me to stand up for myself and take my life back. He poured into me and continued to motivate me, encourage me, inspire me and build me up while putting up with my many shortcomings This is nothing but sheer unconditional love. His support began to elevate my mindset. Gradually I emerged, free and liberated, with a strong and powerful voice. What a beautiful moment!

The next morning finds me settled on my flight. My stomach is a bit queasy, but I am having a nice warm cup of green tea with lemon, no sugar. (I am working to detoxify myself in more ways than one.) We are 36,000 feet in the air. The flight is not bad ... no turbulence. We should touch down in another 20 minutes at Detroit Metropolitan Wayne County Airport.

It has been awhile, I must say. When I left Detroit and moved to Arkansas, I didn't look back. But now I must face my past if I intend to support others on their journey. I cannot be the appointed if I do not possess or understand the tools GOD has given me. So, I must return to the beginning, and change the circumstances.

There is no time to waste; court is at 1 p.m. While Marco was instrumental in awakening me, he has traveled as far as he could to get me here. He can't go in with me, but being the protector that he is, he will stay close by. He's been a pillar of strength, helping me stay anchored for my court appearance. A queen is indeed powerful, but only as powerful as her king. Likewise, his strength lies in her wholeness, for indeed, only together can man and woman create life. Now I have to take a step further and continue this journey on my own. I cannot take my husband somewhere I had never been.

It's 12:30 p.m., a half-hour before the appointed time. I am in downtown Detroit, standing in front of the courthouse. I have my defense attorney at my side.

This preliminary hearing, my first encounter with the legal system, is the setting for what will be the battle of my life. The first step in the process is for the judge to hear both sides of the story. The prosecutor believes she has compelling evidence that will surely convict me of all the crimes of which I'm accused. But I know different. I have years of information that I carefully prepared for this day.

Typically, there are no witnesses until the actual trial, but this is no ordinary trial, no ordinary prosecution nor defense. As I walk through the corridor and through the courtroom square, looking into the courtroom itself, I see a faceless panel. I peer at the panel to determine whether there are any familiar faces, but the area is too dimly lit. Here come my rattled nerves! Will I — or can I — win? This is no ordinary playground. Whatever happens here decides my fate. There are so many pieces of my life that were fractured beyond repair. I wonder if I have enough of a fight in me to bring home a victory.

As the hearing begins, I sit in court, frozen. To me, the prosecuting attorney sounds like the adults in the old Peanut cartoons ... "Whamp, Whamp, Whamp, Whaaaaamp!" I have to get focused,

I tell myself. This is crucial. This will set the stage for my healing, my ministry, my purpose and my calling.

My mental courtroom

The courtroom of my mind is also dimly lit ... not the typical setting. In this courtroom I am poised to fight for the identity of which I have been accused of being undeserving.

In this courtroom, the prosecuting attorney is standing before the members of the jury. These are the people who have found me guilty; their decision has caused me to fall deep into an abyss. I am on the stand, desperately trying to present a compelling argument to save my life. But I am struck down by each member of the jury. One by one they stand and condemn me, each a representation of a broken form of justice. "All I want is to be loved," I say pleadingly.

The attorney here is a legal representation of the members of the jury. But who will stand for me in this mess? For far too long, I have had nothing to say. How will I be vindicated?

As the prosecutor continues to call upon each of those who are convicting me, and as I sit and watch, desperately trying to see the faces of those who are casting their stones of lies, I realize there is a parallel battle, an internal one. In this battle, I am my own prosecutor. The enemy within is always trying to convict me through my own lies about myself. *Is it the truth?* I wonder. *Am I really that bad? Is what they say about me true?*

I cry out to the Most High: "GOD — Your Honor — You know my truth!"

But what would it take for me to realize that MY truth is the truth? What would it take for me to be naked and not ashamed? I have spent my entire life relentlessly struggling to find the truth. I have constantly tried to step away from myself, because the pain and realities of "myself" are overwhelming. And my accusers think they have enough evidence to convict me. They believe I am guilty and for the longest time, I've believed them all. Therefore, constantly fighting this battle within and believing I have no worth, I feel that am nothing.

But I know, in my heart, that this is wrong. *I cannot be this worthless, lying, untrustworthy person against whom all have come to cast judgment,* I tell myself. *I am a beautiful woman, a good mother and wife, and an excellent servant to my GOD.*

I must start asking myself the question that burns inside me, the same question GOD asked Adam and Eve after they ate the forbidden fruit in Genesis 3:11: "Who told you that you are naked?" In other words: Who are you listening to? The members of the jury have their own belief system, and I'd believed their truth rather than honor my own. I'd believed I should be ashamed of my past, my shortcomings. I'd believed that the mistakes I'd made in my life needed to be covered up, while they wanted to expose them. I was so full of shame and guilt over the thoughts they had toward me. GOD had told me in His Word — Jeremiah 29:11 — "For I know the thoughts that I think toward you ... thoughts of peace, and not of evil, to give you an expected end" (KJV). But the cares of this world had choked that Word out of me. I'd been living in a dark cloud of depression, self-hate and thoughts of suicide. My "jury" had taught me to hate *me* because they had judged me so harshly.

Family, "friends," even the church — which was supposed to love me unconditionally — were among my accusers. I just wanted to be loved. I wanted to prove to the jury that I was not the person they accused me of being. But to do that, I had to gather evidence. I needed to believe what the Word says: that I was predestined and that GOD, who had begun a good work in me, would finish what He started (Philippians 1:6).

So, I willingly took the journey to gather evidence to prove my case; to prove that everything my accusers, and I, had believed about me was lies. I also wanted my accusers to know that it was OK for them to uncover me too.

In my mental courtroom, my fear of lying under oath had increased, and had therefore caused more attacks by the jury. They did not want the truth revealed, because that would mean guilt and shame for *them*. But that did not matter. What mattered was that I had evidence that the things my GOD said about me were true. His Word is, and always will be, what I believe.

Are you like me? Did you initially believe the lies the enemy within fed you, fed to others about you ... but then sense deep down that there had to be more to the story? Take the journey through these pages with me to gather evidence contrary to those lies as I face every fear created via my thoughts and my life experiences in my quest to prove my identity.

Chapter Two
I Can't CHANGE What I'm Not Willing to CONFRONT

I can't change what I'm not willing to confront.

What does she mean? you may be wondering. Hmmm ... Where do I start?

First, I must be honest with myself, which is the first step in the healing process. The knowledge that my story is being written reminds me that I am responsible for my own success.

What is my interpretation of success? Let me see. Success is found in attitude and effort. Failure comes only through lack of effort. I have tried over and over to be successful in life, only to experience what I assumed to be failure. So, I suppose I need to remove the word "try" or, at best, the very concept of it. Oftentimes the word "try" is followed by a failed attempt. What's that childhood expression you always hear? "If at first you don't succeed, try, try again." My interpretation of a try was merely an excuse to fail subconsciously.

I had been unaware of the downward spiral that had pulled me further away from achieving success. How I lived my life was indeed a direct reflection of decisions I'd made. My plight was due to no one's actions other than my own.

But, despite many failed tries, and despite my mental/spiritual bondage, I never gave up. "Christel, just quit already. Stop trying to fix your life. You're wasting time here," I would say, trying to convince myself to throw in the towel. On the other hand, I knew this was wrong, and I'd end up having this mental battle with myself. As time moved on, I gained strength, embraced self-confidence and told myself, "Christel, do me a favor. Just *do* the damn thing! Fix your life!"

To revisit my past and deal with all the emotions I suppressed was difficult, painful and sometimes sickening. It took a lot of prayer. I have wanted to tell my story for three years now. but I'd been so full of fear, anxiety and worry that I would start and stop, start and stop. Not this time! I'm going all the way.

As I'd Been Taught

Could it be

That I parented myself

The way my parents parented me?

My mom worked all the time

I worked all the time

My mom put others before me

I put others before me

She sacrificed me

I sacrificed myself

She didn't listen to me

I didn't trust or listen to myself

She provided

I've worked to provide

My dad said I was ugly

I've felt ugly

My dad chose others before me

I chose others before me

My dad provided support only

I provide support

My father was passive

I was passive

My parents didn't express themselves

I didn't express myself

My feelings never mattered

So I suppressed instead of expressed

Have you ever said, "I'm not going to be anything like my mother or father"? I did. You guessed it: I turned out just like them.

My mother could only reproduce what she was. Well, who was she? She was once a broken, rejected woman. Growing up, she rarely heard the words "I love you" and she struggled with feelings of abandonment. She didn't have a voice. She rarely expressed what she was feeling; in fact, I never saw my mother cry. Molested as a young girl, she told no one ... and was left feeling unprotected. She married my father early, then stayed in that marriage for 11 unhappy years because she thought staying would change her husband. She eventually divorced and stayed in a long-term relationship before remarrying, this time to her first love. Unfortunately, she ended up in the same cycle in which she'd been trapped during her first marriage. This time, she thought her faith would change her husband. The second marriage lasted nearly as long as the first. One day, she woke up and realized she deserved better. Courageously, she did what she had to do for *her*.

Despite her past struggles, my mother loves with everything in her, and serves others unconditionally. She extends herself for anyone in need. That's what GOD created her to be ... love. She'd spent years searching for something *outside* of her, when all she desired and needed was *within* her.

My story is so much like my mother's. I grew up feeling rejected because I was different ... tall, with big feet, and big for my age in general. I often lied about my age because people would be shocked when they heard how young I was for my looks. I had abandonment issues because my dad wasn't around. I had no voice, because when I used it, it wasn't heard. I was molested. I married early, stayed for 17 years because I thought I could change my husband, divorced, then married a second time to my first love. I am my mother's daughter. In earlier times, young people were not taught to look within themselves for love. My mother could only take me as far as she had been taken. And everything she was, I became.

I'll briefly discuss my father. I say "briefly" because we didn't establish a real relationship until I was older. My father was not a communicator; he was a very passive man, and the only time he had a lot to say was after he'd had a few drinks. I asked both my mother and stepmother about my father and I found it very interesting that their experiences with him, major and minor, were quite similar. When it came time for my mother to give birth to me, for instance, my dad dropped her off at the hospital, went to park the car, and stayed gone so long that he missed my delivery. He did the same thing with my stepmother when she gave birth to my half-brother. Here were two different women who'd experienced the same treatment from the same emotionally distant man.

I was everything my mother *and* father were. My mother carried and delivered me, the bondwoman; it was up to me to take the journey to be baptized to become a free woman. All old things must pass away and all things must become new. How would this baptism take place? I had to go back to the womb, not physically but spiritually. I had to visit the dark places of my soul so that the Spirit could lead me to the truth, back to the seed from which I/we were originally created … the seed of love. That's the treasure hidden in our earthen vessel. If you're going to find it, you must dig.

Where is the love?

My mother had two children — my brother; then, 11 years later, me. Just as she didn't get hugs or I-love-yous from her mother, we didn't get them from her. She worked long hours to provide for us, and she met our material needs, which was a demonstration of her love. But I wanted more than that. I wanted my mother's time and attention. Work had her time. Her long-term boyfriend, who came into my life when I was 2, had her attention.

Now we did things as a family; my mother and her boyfriend took us and his children to amusement parks and other destinations. But communication didn't exist in our home … that is, not until my brother or I got in trouble with my mother; then, the communication was discipline-related. This made me resent my mom. The media portrays a mother as someone who nurtures her children, communicates with them, and does things with them. As a little girl, seeing my mother working all those hours and not experiencing what the media had shown me, I felt unloved, rejected and abandoned in my own home. It didn't help when my father failed to show up to pick me up when scheduled to do so, or chose my stepmother over me.

I felt that I needed to be someone else in order to be loved. These feelings worsened at the age of 12, when I experienced the trauma I will recount a bit later … trauma that robbed me of my identity.

At the age of 13, I began my journey to find the identity I would take on to receive love and acceptance. Inevitably, I began having sex with multiple partners. Initially, this felt good to me because I had accepted the false truth that sex was love and that I had to sacrifice myself to gain what I'd sought. Now prostitution is what it's called when you get paid for having illicit sex with someone. The only "pay" I ever received was, as the old saying goes, a wet behind. That, and the very temporary filling of the void that was in me.

As a matter of fact, the love I sought was never freely given in *any* of my childhood or adolescent relationships; I always had to give something to get it. Those who I thought were my friends accepted me only if I did what they were doing. I was an honor-roll student, but the other children made fun of me and ostracized me for being smart and standing out. So, I dimmed my light and became *them*.

One day, my so-called friends encouraged me to skip school and go to the mall. I decided to go, not thinking of the consequences, just about how good it felt to be wanted and accepted. As we walked through the mall, laughing, I saw this tall, light-complexioned, bowlegged and very attractive young man eyeing me. *Is he looking at me?* I wondered with excitement. I could see he was quite a bit older than my 13 years. But, oh, was he ever fine, and he was looking at *me*!

My admirer approached me, giving me a look that I would never forget. It almost felt like I was in a trance. We talked, exchanged numbers, and from then on, we were inseparable. I became his "ride-or-die" chick. On weekends, I would meet him at my godsister's house, where I had the freedom and liberty to do "grown-up" stuff.

At some point I found out that my boyfriend was involved with other girls, which meant I was left feeling abandoned again. So, my search for love continued. There was another young man who would visit the people living next door to my godsister. He was really digging me ... and I was digging him, because he gave me the attention I so longed for. It was then — again, I was only 13 — that I concluded that I would have to keep a backup boyfriend so that I wouldn't feel rejected or abandoned again. Because I identified sex as love, keeping both boyfriends meant that I had to sleep with them both.

Not surprisingly, my search for love and acceptance left me pregnant at the age of 14. The boyfriend I assumed to be the father was not, I found out much later.

I gave birth to my firstborn after I turned 15. He became my lifeline. I finally had someone who loved and accepted me and would never leave me! He was mine, and I was his. I remember sitting on my bed, holding my son, singing "Thanks for My Child," that old R&B song by Cheryl "Pepsii" Riley about an unwed mother. My son was my motivation to live a life that was different from the one I'd been living. Although I did live differently, I struggled at times. I went from being a teenager to being a mom, which means that I didn't get to experience what teenagers normally experience. I had to go to school, work and take care of my son.

Chapter Three

Wanting to be Heard, but Having Lost My Voice:

My Mother's Daughter

Have you ever wanted to question things you have been taught your entire life, but feared that your questioning would make you sound ignorant?

Have you ever wanted to share a word or a revelation with someone, but feared their lack of understanding? Their judgment?

Have you ever wanted to give someone a piece of your mind, but held back for fear of hurting that person's feelings?

Have you ever wanted to share something private with your parents, but were afraid they would look at you differently after you did?

Have you ever wanted very, very much to let someone know that you were being treated inappropriately — but remained silent because you'd been warned that you "bet" not tell and you were afraid of the discord you may cause if you did?

Have you ever wanted to end a relationship with someone, but stayed in the relationship due to fear or low self-esteem?

Have you ever?

In my case, the answer to every question is a Yes. I had opportunities to express what I was feeling, but I kept those feelings to myself because of my fear of being judged, misunderstood, rejected. If you're anything like me, you probably understand exactly why I never used my voice. If not, dig deeper here in order to understand.

Today, I'm a seeker of truth. But I was a young girl in a grown woman's body when I first began asking myself many truth-seeking questions: *Why won't you stand up for yourself? Why do you let people treat you any kind of way?* The answers to these questions were always within me ... but they resided in the deepest, darkest places within. Seeking and uncovering those answers would indeed be uncomfortable, but I knew I had to do it.

I began my search by seeking my own voice and trying to discover just why I hadn't been vocal about the things that mattered the most to me.

I lost my voice

Imagine a 12-year girl sick at home with a high fever, itching with the chicken pox while her mom is working a 12-hour shift.

Her chicken pox has begun to spread all over her breasts, between her legs, and down her back. The girl is being attended to by her mom's boyfriend, a frequent visitor to the home. Now this man is no stranger to the girl; he has been around ever since she was 2 years old, and he is like a dad to her. This man has literally watched her grow into a young lady. She has trusted him … until this day, when he touches her in places he shouldn't. Can you imagine this? I can, because she was me. I was that 12-year old girl, with a 12-year-old mind, but the body of a 16-year old and a bra size of about 34C.

I remember that day at our home in Detroit as though it were yesterday. That morning, my mom gave her boyfriend, whom I'll call Joe, instructions to put calamine lotion on my back to soothe the chicken pox. Still in my sickbed, I awakened to overhear the command, and since Momma didn't play, I didn't dare consider disobeying. So, when Joe came into my bedroom a little later with the lotion, I lifted my shirt for him.

I handed him the lotion and he began to rub my back in a way that made me very uncomfortable. I remember closing my eyes tightly, terrified because I didn't know what was going to happen next. As he rubbed my back, I felt his hands come around to my sides. I froze as his hands moved to my breasts, which he cupped very firmly, then began to caress them as I pleaded with him several times to stop.

I eventually broke away and ran into a corner of the kitchen, dropping to the floor and curling up as deeply as I could ... shaking, trembling, crying and hoping someone would come home and save me. Joe ambled in, sat down at the kitchen table, stared at me in the corner.

"You bet' not tell," he finally said. "She's not going to believe you anyway."

I looked at him in disbelief and felt not only fear, but pure disgust as he told me to pull my pants down. He said he would pay me $5 dollars for every hair I had between my legs.

I jumped up, not knowing what was about to happen, and ran to a friend's house. I stayed there until almost time for my mother to come home. Exhausted from the horrific day, I returned home. While Joe listened to old-school music and sipped his brown liquor in the living room, I sneaked into my mother's room, locked myself in there and fell asleep.

Some time later, I was awakened by something hard pressing against my back. I felt Joe's arm reach around to grab me. I jumped up and ran off again, this time into the basement, where I crouched on the floor and cried.

His words began to play over and over in my mind: *She's not going to believe you.* I wanted to use my voice, but I was afraid Joe might be right.

About an hour or so later, my mother arrived. Relieved and afraid at the same time, I tried to assure myself that she was going to kick Joe's behind when I told her what he'd done to me. Being the clean and organized woman that she was, I counted on her making her weekly trip into the basement to iron clothes. I couldn't wait for her to come downstairs so that I could tell her about the hell into which I'd been plunged.

Fear tried to creep in again. *No, Christel, you cannot stay quiet. This is going to get worse and worse*, I told myself.

Sure enough, my mother come downstairs. She stopped when she saw me on the floor.

It took me a few seconds for me to get the words out. "Momma, I need to tell you something and I really need you to believe me."

Staring, she asked what it was that I needed to tell her. Gathering up every ounce of courage, I continued.

"Momma, your boyfriend has been touching me in my private areas and he offered me money for the number of hairs between my legs. He put his privates up against my back and — "

She rushed towards me, waving her hand for me to stop sharing. "Girl, quit lying. You are just trying to manipulate me!"

What?! I thought. *Manipulate you?! My momma?!*

I implored her to believe me, but her only response was, "Go to your room."

I was broken. Crushed. I'd been molested, and I wasn't being heard. Joe was right — she didn't believe me. Can you imagine my inner trauma? Can you fathom the disbelief I felt at the realization that my mother would sacrifice her only daughter for a man — *this* man?

This became the day I lost my voice.

Not only did my mother choose to stay with Joe; we moved into his home. I had to accept my mother's boyfriend because this is who she chose to be with. And, living in his home, I had to face him … every single day.

Joe and my mother's bedroom was upstairs. I slept in a room downstairs, keeping my door locked in hopes of avoiding any more unwanted encounters with Joe. (I also began going to bed with my clothes on.)

But I knew I wouldn't be able to keep myself safe forever.

One morning, I had to go up to their room to get something. Momma was in the shower, so I called to her to let her know I was there. "I'll be out shortly," she said.

On the way downstairs, I encountered Joe. He tapped me on my arm.

"Don't you hate you told?" he asked.

At that moment, I knew I'd better tell somebody else what Joe had done before things got worse. That's when I told my brother, who, being 11 years older, was now a young adult living elsewhere. My brother told my mother that if she didn't get me out of that house, he was going to call Child Protective Services on her.

That's how I got out of the situation ... well, physically. We moved out of Joe's house, but my mother kept seeing him. Her mind and heart were still with him.

She and Joe continued to see each other for some years. Today he's still in Michigan, with a family of his own.

Initially, I trusted this man because he was someone my mother trusted. When he molested me, I didn't realize that that trauma I sustained from that event would play out in so many parts of my life, well into my adulthood. Here I am now, in my 40s, and still not fully expressing myself, or even *wanting* to be heard, for fear of the unknown.

Blind, Deaf and mute

I later found out that my mother had suffered her own molestation trauma. She once told me that she didn't even remember me telling her about Joe. In truth, her trauma had her so closed off that she couldn't bear to be reminded of it.

And I followed in her footsteps, becoming a child sacrifice because she did not know how to respond to what I had told her about her man. When she was molested as a child, she, too, had been afraid of not being heard. Staying quiet, pretending nothing happened, became her truth. Her sacrifice of me, when it happened to me, caused me to lose my voice, just as she had lost hers. Her refusal to believe my molestation must go back to something I did or didn't do, I concluded. This aggravated my insecurity, my feeling of not being enough. So, I didn't speak at all … not about what was right; not about what was wrong; not about anything else. I just went with the flow. My entire life became built on lies and faulty trust in others, even when I knew *their* truth to be ugly.

Not only did I lose my voice, I was programmed to remain loyal to dysfunctional relationships, as my mother had. Therefore, I remained loyal to a number of relationships that I should have cut loose but held onto despite their toxicity. These relationships included the dysfunctional marriage in which I remained for 17 years. I'm not saying that the 17 years were all bad. We connected on a childlike level, but as I grew mature, I realized I was holding on to the *idea* of a man being present in my life rather than what I really needed. (I always say, however, that my programming was both a curse and a blessing. Yes, I stayed in bad relationships. But I also had the gift of being longsuffering, sticking with those who needed me to tarry with them as I ministered to them.)

As I grew into adulthood, I often wondered why I felt stuck, felt that life was just passing me by. I was blind, deaf *and* mute:

Blind — I couldn't see or experience love because I was blinded by my past experiences, which robbed me of the truth. When GOD sent individuals to love me, I didn't know how to receive that love because it was foreign to me. I couldn't see a reason *why* they loved me. My vision was distorted by my past.

Deaf — I lost my trust in GOD somewhere along my journey, and I no longer trusted what the Spirit was speaking to me because I couldn't hear Him properly. Instead I trusted others, listening to what *they* said I should be and do.

Mute — I feared not being heard, so I kept a closed mouth. I used sign language and my actions to communicate my needs and desires. The hurt, lack of fulfillment, and lack of joy had driven me into a deep pit. By trying to use a language that no one truly understood, including myself, my communication with others and myself was way off. People had no clue what I was trying to express; they hadn't taken my life course, so their lack of understanding resulted in the further diminishment of my self-worth and self-acceptance. I felt for years that people were constantly taking from me. Granted, there are those who will take from people as long as they're giving, and I have had my share of those. But some of the people in my life simply failed to understand me because I didn't understand myself. My mother's failure to hear me caused me to believe that other people's words mattered more than my own because theirs were the words she listened to.

Welcome Home

What did I learn from home?

What I experienced from home externally

Is where I learned some of my internal behaviors.

No attention (I wasn't a priority)

Busy (I didn't matter)

To be homeless

Wandering, searching for a place to live

I lived at Alcohol Street

Promiscuity Street

Religion Station

Validation Complex.

Home is where the heart is.

Where is your heart?

Home is supposed to be a place where

you experience love, learn and grow.

Home is where you feel safe and protected,

Sure, and accepted.

I didn't get any of those things at home.

So if home is where the heart is,

where is my heart?

There's no place like home.

Well subconsciously, home was not a safe place,

it was not a place

where you felt love, peace, security, protection ...

and so I've been running from home. Running from me. My physical experience had robbed me and caused my head and heart to run in different directions.

But it's time to come back home, head and heart in alignment.

I began asking myself these questions

Why don't you want to go home?

What are you running from?

What are you afraid of?

It's safe to come home

after 40 years of running.

Within your home as a child

is where you learn love and acceptance.

Within my home

I learned the opposite.

When you're blind, deaf and mute — physically, mentally or spiritually — it's difficult for you to do anything without assistance. I can say, however, that GOD was my anchor back then ... as He is now. He kept me, throughout and despite my mess.

(Let me pause here to say this: If you experienced several molestation incidents, as I had, you may have tried to diminish or dismiss what happened to you. You may have told yourself that you came out "good" in comparison to others who experienced long-term molestation, rape or other forms of sexual abuse, or other forms of physical abuse at the hands of parents, stepparents, boyfriends or girlfriends of parents, uncles, older siblings, cousins, family friends or trusted childhood group leaders. Do not dismiss your trauma just because it may not have been as "serious" as another's. You may not have undergone abuse to the same degree or duration as others have, but you underwent abuse ... abuse that went on to serve as an ever-present cloud over your life, keeping you from getting the sunlight — or, if you will, the Son Light, JESUS.)

Eventually I gained the ability to communicate by *receiving* and *feeling*, as well as seeing, hearing and yes, speaking. It was a process: I had to see myself as someone greater than my past experiences, someone who deserved love. As my sight developed, so did my hearing ... and my voice.

Yes, I found my voice. It was funny ... my voice was unrecognizable at first. Hearing it, I felt like a newborn infant hearing her mother's voice for the first time once out of the womb: The sound is strange to the baby at first, but then she begins to realize that it's familiar to her. When I began speaking, I was in disbelief. I asked myself whether it was really me talking. *Could it be GOD? Could it be someone else?* I wondered. For so long, I'd had more of a belief in others than in myself. I believed in *their* ideas about GOD and ignored what I believed to be true. I accepted *their* truth as my own instead of seeking GOD for, and by, myself. I had to learn to listen to my voice as well as the right external voices. I had to find the right connections and begin to trust what I was hearing. It was GOD's calling on my life to be my True Self.

Then, I had to start *moving*. I had to move into the things I wanted to do. And I had to learn to *trust* again ... not only other people, but myself.

It was the enemy's plan to steal my voice a long time ago, and it is the enemy's plan to steal your voice as well. But there's a saying: "You can't curse what GOD has already blessed." I had to believe that I, the person He'd created me to be since before I was formed in my mother's womb, was enough.

When you seek, you will find clues, then answers. Once I found the clues, I was able to trace them back to find my voice. I was able to hear once more what the spirit was saying to "my" church, which is all of me. I began to receive the things that would be required of me in order for me to take this journey. I had to face my fears, move forward, and be willing to be uncomfortable no matter the cost. We each must obey if we are ever going to find our True Self and uncover the treasure within.

Chapter Four
Unconscious Seeds (Twins)

S elf-rejection and low self-worth are the twins that lived in my subconscious. I call them twins because these two hang out together.

Your subconscious reality is created by stored information … information of which you sometimes aren't even aware. When my mother delivered me, she appeared awake, but she was mentally asleep. She went through life playing out what she'd seen and become used to, acting automatically according to her previous experiences and the expectations that grew from them. Then, when I was born, I was able to play out only what I had seen.

To stop repeating a cycle, you must question certain things about yourself to find out whether the life you're living is based on your truth, or the truth that's been handed down to you. I wasn't aware that the twins, self-rejection and low self-worth, existed until they showed up in my life. I believed these twins belonged to me. I nurtured and took care of them. I provided them with everything they needed to survive. I fed them through my thoughts, words and life experiences. I accepted these twins as mine instead of the twins that were meant to be mine – self-acceptance and self-love. I spent 40 years holding self-rejection and low self-worth close. All they did in return was make me feel useless and unworthy of anything good. I gave and gave and gave … only to be taken, again and again and again.

One day I began to reflect, wondering how I'd become so bitter and so full of resentment, guilt and shame. I began to look closely at the twins. I came to realize that they looked nothing like me, but they did resemble some folks in my family. I guess that's why I recognized them and never questioned whether they were really mine. When I began having conversations with the twins, I realized that they didn't *sound* like they belonged to me. I'd been afraid of abandoning them; I'd held onto them as long as I could because I thought my job was to protect and serve them.

I began asking myself some hard questions, the chief of which was: Where had the original twins, self-acceptance and self-love, gone? Both sets of twins remained within me. But it was the set I'd nurtured and fed that were the most dominant. I had to starve self-rejection and low self-worth, and feed self-acceptance and self-love. I'd spent 40 years feeding the wrong twins. How? With thoughts, which are seeds. I planted those seeds in my heart and reproduced what never belonged to me. When I finally got the courage to face my fears of abandonment and rejection, I had to adopt a new belief about my twins. I had to believe that the *me* who GOD had created was enough. I had to believe that I was accepted and worthy.

I could no longer ignore the truth. I no longer cared about feeding what didn't belong to me. I had to abort the negative thoughts, words and actions I'd reproduced ... thoughts, words and actions that had been reproduced earlier by my mother and grandmother (generational curses). I needed to feed self-acceptance and self-love if I was ever going to be my True Self.

In one of his Facebook posts, California author, pastor and spiritual coach Patrick Weaver wrote that "sometimes you have to sit in your feelings in order to understand why you have to stand on your truth." Feelings, according to Weaver, tell the truth about beliefs that may be lies or lie-based, so to get to the bottom of our feelings, we must scrutinize our beliefs: "Emotions are based on your beliefs — true or false. Feelings narrate your beliefs. Thoughts respond to your feelings. Behavior acts out your thoughts."

Weaver went on to point out that "sometimes false feelings will put a period where GOD meant for you to put a comma, and sometimes feelings will put a question mark where GOD meant for you to put a period ... Sometimes joy, right thoughts and even wisdom is held hostage by wrong feelings." He urged readers to validate their feelings in order to walk in their truth.

OK ... so what does that mean? Accepting me as I truly am? Exactly who am I — truly?

That's what I used to ask myself. I couldn't determine who I was in order to *accept* me as I was. (I realize this sounds a lot like me running game on me ... straight double-talk.) I had become everything that everyone else needed and wanted me to be. I was never taught to look at myself first for acceptance. Therefore, my experiences, relationships and the lies I told myself created an identity called "not good enough." I would walk around, pleasing and appeasing others while neglecting me. It was all for the satisfaction of others ... their gains, at my expense.

The person I saw in the mirror was trapped beyond words. Each day, she would look back at me with sadness and dismay. I would cry inside, feeling as trapped as the image I cast. I wondered if there would ever come a time when I would finally be free; when I'd be able to step through that looking glass and embrace the vision there: myself. In light of all the drama and pain cast upon me, I felt it was safe to keep "self" tucked away, behind the mirror reflection, to avoid pain.

They say that when we look at people, we see in them the qualities that match our own. Through the laws of attraction, we gravitate to people who have traits that are similar to ours, and we become their mirror image. I was in need of acceptance, so

I was connected to people who were broken like me — some were in *worse* shape. I reasoned that they would not reject me because they were just as much in need of fixing as I. So, I would oftentimes become the sacrifice in an effort to protect them from experiencing those same feelings I had ... feelings of rejection, abandonment and worthlessness.

Clearly the person I saw in the mirror was in deep anguish and was ready to break free. Not to dwell on the mirror, but it does make you think. The mirror can be a tricky device, often causing distorted perceptions depending on how you look into it. In my case it was I, trying to discover me, who would finally decide it was time to take off the mask. My mask was made up of judgments and illusions from myself and all the people around me.

None of my relationships up to this point in my life had been what I desired them to be. I fought so hard to be accepted by my family and friends. Failed relationships with family can be especially hurtful. We tend to harbor certain expectations about family ... about them loving us, supporting us, encouraging us, celebrating us, lifting us up. When we don't get that, it can be heartbreaking. I wondered at times whether there something wrong with me, something that caused my family to pay me no attention. I worked hard and sacrificed for them because I, just being *me*, wasn't enough.

Where did this lie come from, this lie that I wasn't enough? It was created in my mind as a result of my life experiences. Well, guess what? Even after all my accomplishments, nothing changed. Family still paid me no attention.

I had to come to terms with what I was being shown, over and over again: that I needed to accept my family for who they are and accept the choice some of them had made to not be part of my life. Yes, it was a hard pill to swallow. Their actions made me want to distance myself from them. I didn't want to believe I didn't have the perfect family, but if I was ever going to be free from my pain, I had to let go. Letting go isn't easy, but it's worth it. I let go of my idea of who, what and how I wanted them to be, and received with open arms those who chose to be a part of my life. In confronting the lie that my family was perfect, I had to accept my responsibility in the perpetuation of that lie: My family was the same as they'd always been. I'd told myself they should be something else; then, when they proved not to be who I thought they should be, my insecurities kicked in and I took it personally. In other words, they were being themselves — and I was playing the victim. My playing the victim always made it appear that something was being done *to* me instead of *for* me. My thoughts created the reality I lived in. When we accept responsibility for our lives, we stop playing the blame game. We are where we are in life because of what we believe.

Unrealistic, and unfulfilled, expectations in my family relationships were just one manifestation of the "I'm not enough" attitude playing out in my life. These expectations came up in other relationships also.

Here is a for-instance: I became angry at a friend for not being the sister to me that I had been to her. Examining my anger more closely, I realized that this woman wasn't really looking for a sister; she wanted a mentor. That's actually how our relationship had begun, but I'd shifted the relationship. Operating from my unresolved issues, I had overreacted to my friend's casual reference to me as "sister" and therefore, overextended myself. When we allow people to put titles on us, we may be taking on a role we never auditioned for. Given the title of "sister," I did what sisters do … love, support, sacrifice … because, as the old pop hit goes, "we are family." At least, that's what *I* desired in a family, but my friend's experience was different. She did not reciprocate in kind. I could have blamed her for my overextension, but she didn't force me to accept the sister role in which I expected reciprocity. With titles come expectations, based on the individual. In most cases, it's unspoken expectation, which lead to disappointment.

I accepted responsibility and apologized to her for not accepting her for who she was. I even wrote her a letter. It read:

Hey, friend!

Let me first apologize by [stepping out of] the role as mentor in your life and shifting the relationship into something personal. I expected something from you that you weren't even looking for [from me]. You weren't looking for a sister or a family; however, because of what I wanted, I tried to make you something that you didn't even sign up for. I apologize. [My family and I gave to] you from our hearts, [but then], we expected the same in return instead of accepting you as you are. You have every right to pursue your goals and dreams and should never put them on the back burner for anyone.

However, I do believe that if you truly value the relationship [you have with someone], then you will also consider them sometimes before yourself, because that's what family does. I got a reality check the day of your procedure when you said you and [your] Mom had a great day [and] that's the way family is supposed to be, not just when you need something ... I realized then that maybe your eyes were opening, and maybe not. Either way, I had to support and accept you where you are — without an expectation ... I am releasing you of all expectations, and going forward, I accept and support you as you are. I love you and only want what's best for you and your family. Please accept my apology.

I love you always,

Christel

Another for-instance: As a young girl, I looked for a mother figure in several women. Again, I craved the attention, affection, validation and nurturing a mother usually gives her daughter but that I had not received. So, I "adopted" these women, calling them Mom and trying to fill an emotional void they didn't know existed. I would eventually blame each woman for not giving me what I needed, and I would end the relationship. I even addressed my pastor as "Mom" and became angry when I didn't get the attention and affirmation I felt she should have given me. I went to her, too, and asked for forgiveness because I was harboring resentment toward her. I wanted to be loved. I wanted to be accepted. I wanted to be heard. I wanted to be seen for who I was, not for what I could do. These women had no idea what I wanted and needed, but I expected them to give it to me.

This also happened with men, whom I'd adopt as "brother" or "dad" in my attempts to fill the void of a male presence in my life. My emotional needs led to disappointment after disappointment after disappointment.

My internal programming had to change. According to what Pastor Weaver had written, I had to confront, with truth, the lies on which my feelings were based. I had to accept me, love me, and support who I was becoming. But I couldn't do it without downloading new programming ... I AM ENOUGH. I AM ENOUGH. I AM ENOUGH!

My Brokenness

He was my mirror

and embodied everything I no longer wanted to be

and everything I needed to be.

The things he reflected were ugly

and the more I saw it,

the more I wanted to break that mirror.

So I threw words at it.

I threw anger, resentment,

and, at times, thoughts of hatred and suicide.

I did everything to destroy my mirror

but he stood and he stood.

There was no breaking this mirror.

My experiences were designed to break me,

but love was then, and is now, my anchor.

I couldn't recognize the anchor within myself,

but I eventually recognized it in him ... my mirror,

the mirror I wanted to destroy.

He was consistent, determined

and dedicated to revealing the truth.

My experiences had defined me and trapped me,

but his unconditional love saved and healed me.

I am thankful for my mirror

and what GOD placed in him.

He was determined to love me back to the real me.

Love truly overrules all things

and draws you from that unhealthy place.

All I could see was the other me,

butt all he could see was the real me.

He is my selfless, understanding, genuine ... Angel. My S.U.G.A.

Chapter Five
Archetype to My Survival: The Orphans of My Soul

The prostitute in me was one that was always so submissive, always giving of self. I gave, thinking I would get something back. The prostitute within me was so broken, so in need of love, affection and attention. I did not place value within; therefore, I made deals with pimps.

Now just how does she define "pimp"? you may be asking.

The pimp label could apply to any number of people in your space. Your pimp could be your momma, your daughter, your boss. The only reason they are in your life, pimpin' you, is because you are giving them something! You give, hoping to get something in return, but you don't. Love and relationships do, by nature, have a give-and-take dynamic; ideally, both participants are giving. But in an uneven relationship, one party is doing the giving. I gave parts of my soul in hopes of receiving. I thought I had to be loved in order to be whole — there was that prosecutor again, filling my head with those damned lies. And while my pimps indicated that I would receive, all they did was take, take, take. I gave of myself until there was nothing more to give.

I didn't believe I was enough just as I was. I didn't think my personality alone made me worthy of receiving love. I believed love, affection and attention had to be worked for. So, I suffered and humiliated myself at times just to receive a little affection. Whenever someone nice offered me love, I suspected their love to be fake because I hadn't earned it. I would self-sabotage, not even realizing it, and run real love away because of the depth of the wounds that existed within me. If I was ever going to experience the true love I desired, I had to accept the love that CHRIST freely gave. I could no longer accept what I *thought* love was, based on my personal experiences.

My idea of having to work for love changed when my self-perception changed. My old perception had created the illusion that I wasn't enough. My perception today says I *am* enough, and I *can* and *will* receive love that is given freely.

In the court of my mind — the court in which I had to fight for the identity of which I'd been robbed — it became clear that my accuser had a lifetime journal on me that was full of lies. I had to put my argument together to defend myself. The prosecutor surely had me pegged as a cheap trick, because I was always wheeling and dealing and selling myself. Who does that? Well … in this case … me. Thank GOD, I eventually woke up and decided I wasn't going to be anyone's prostitute anymore. I wasn't "uppin' it" anymore.

Now we know what happens if you're a prostitute and you don't pay your pimp. He starts whipping your behind. But when you stand up and refuse to allow him or anyone else to control you, all that "pimp madness" goes out the front door. See, when you take your power back, the people using you start to get angry and start acting out. Why? Because their benefits are coming to a screeching halt. If you are doing what they want you to do, it's all good. You've seen this behavior, right? You may have a friend like that in your life right now. I'm here to tell you, you'd better drop that zero!

As you find your footing and begin to reclaim your power, the pimps do everything in their powers to dominate and control you once again. They want you back on the corner. They want you to be dependent on them. When you take away that which sustains them, it's an all-out war. So, as I slowly started to *reclaim* my life, I realized I was in the *fight* for my life. I was afraid that if I stepped up and stood up for myself, I would find myself back on that corner again. I was afraid of becoming powerless.

The child in me was looking for a father figure — one who would provide. The child, the prostitute and the victim were all working together with the Archetype. As a child, I assumed that if I did a chore, I would be rewarded. I didn't fully understand that the chore was something I was supposed to do, a responsibility that would shape me as I grew into womanhood.

I was busy doing grown-up things, but I was still so very lost. I was still trying to find my peace, searching for what had been missing in my childhood. Because my daddy never showed me how I was supposed to be treated, I allowed myself to be pimped out repeatedly. And I never questioned it, because I thought I was getting what I needed, which was provision. But it wasn't.

In 1 Corinthians 13:11 in the New Testament, the Apostle Paul writes: "When I was a child, I spake as a child, I understood as a child, I thought as a child: but when I became a man, I put away childish things" (KJV). When I was a child, I was a child; my problem is that when I grew up, I still did childish things. I had been drawn to men I thought I needed to validate me. I would act in childish ways in my attempts to get them to validate me. The victim in me, living the "woe is me" life, had beaten me down. I took on the role of poor, defenseless Christel. And with this behavior, I drew men in my life that caused me to victimize myself. I thought I was OK with it, but I only received temporary satisfaction.

But as I matured in CHRIST, I made the decision to put that old me away.

In the court of my mind, I listen to the characters who step forward and state their false testimonies about me, accusations they'd repeated for years. They are embroiled in heated sidebars as they go back and forth to determine whose truth is most reflective of me. I am shaking my head as I peer into the darkened box, desperately trying to see those who dare to discredit my good name. How dare you cast stones upon me? I think. What's that famous line? People who live in glass houses should never cast stones.

Try as I might, I can't see these accusers. What the accusers did not know is that GOD, the Judge — tall, stately, majestic, and larger than life itself — could see into their souls, but not the reverse. They had no clue as to what ... as to Who... they were up against.

If you are where I once was, you must confront the prosecutor within you. When you do so, fear of man transforms into fear of GOD. You put that fear of GOD before what you once accepted as fate. You put the divine before the physical. When you shift your understanding of why you do what you do, you no longer act as a prostitute.

Sometimes, despite your newfound knowledge that you must fear GOD and take responsibility for yourself, you continue to operate in fear of man and become the saboteur of your fate. Whenever you are presented with an opportunity to do something meaningful with your life, you find yourself unable to progress because you are so busy operating in fear. You know what you need to do, but you don't follow through. You self-sabotage because it is more comfortable to remain that child within. You've prostituted yourself for so long, you become used to operating in your lower self. Often, in this case, you become the very person who victimized you ... in other words, you become the pimp! Crazy, right? You begin to take on pimp characteristics, because you've been around the pimp for such a long time. You begin to act out of your ill-gotten intentions. You begin to manipulate situations to achieve the end results you desire.

Just as you are burdened with this archetype that is drowning you, you can easily become that of which you were once a victim if you're not careful.

My Addiction

My husband had told me that I didn't listen; that I was always defensive. Finally, I asked myself why. I realized it was a symptom of my addiction. I'm addicted to feeling like I'm not enough, so when he is critical of me, I go into denial, unwilling to accept or confront my addiction. Every time I resist the truth of my addiction, I fall deeper into it. With my addiction comes the fear of rejection and abandonment, fear that overtakes me to the point that it makes me sick to my stomach. It's why I defend my position. I ignore the fact that there is a problem that needs to be dealt with, and I pretend I'm OK — that's what addicts do until they're once again confronted about their addiction. Resisting the truth only causes it to persist. The experiences come faster and harder each time until the addict hits rock bottom.

I never wanted to be an addict, but life happened; I got hooked on the notion that I was unworthy and had no value. When you have an addiction to pain, it will rob you of everything you've wanted and worked for. If you're never willing to admit that your experiences have created a dependency, you will spend your entire life looking for that same "hit." And my addiction had robbed me continually of my dreams, goals, finances, health (thanks to an ancillary addiction to food, to which I turned whenever my feelings overwhelmed me), relationships, and purpose.

If I was ever going to take my life back, I had to face what I did, and how I hurt others, in my addiction. I had to accept the truth, regardless of how badly it hurt and how badly I wanted to defend my addiction or hide behind it. Accepting the truth meant facing the fear of rejection and abandonment and trusting the process of being freed from my addiction, once and for all.

My unhealthy attachment (addiction) to the person I used to be also served to sabotage some of my relationships. I would spend too much time focused on the wrong things; as a result, my energy would often be depleted. My relationships weren't healthy because I wasn't healthy. As much as I wanted to believe I had moved on from my issues, I was still presented with the same hard life lessons — an indication that my addiction remained the driving force behind my behavior. I had lost control of my life. Having to admit, accept and deal with this was as painful as identifying myself as an addict. I had to choose my pain: either the pain that would come with my efforts to change, or the pain that would continue if I stayed the same. I choose the pain that came with change. I choose to accept me as I am and accept what I'd done.

Because of this choice, I am no longer a victim of my circumstances; I am now the "shero" in my story. There was no one else on earth that could save me; I had to save myself.

The good news is that once you have accepted the truth that you're an addict, and you share your nakedness with those who truly care about you, they are going to cover you with love, acceptance and encouragement. They are not going to provoke you in any way that will cause you to relapse. The purpose of confessing your addiction is to help others assist you in becoming a healthier, happier you.

Overcoming my addiction started with self-love, self-forgiveness, and self-acceptance. When you love yourself, you quit making *excuses* and you start to make *moves* – life-changing moves. You go to the gym instead of feeding your cravings with cookies, cake, ice cream. When you accept yourself, you're not worried about whether people like you; you know there are those who will like you and accept you as you are.

And, when you forgive yourself, the unforgiveness that once lived within you will no longer be a distraction. Forgiveness is always for you. It's funny how I could give everyone else what I wanted and needed, but could never give it to myself. I'm reminded of how frustrated I once was with my son because he'd remember to practice good manners while away from home, but always needed to be reminded to use them while at home. It's crazy how we will give others the very thing we should be giving ourselves (or, in my son's case, giving those with whom he lived). We owe ourselves the same love and respect we give others. We place more value in them than we do ourselves, then wonder why we are misused, mistreated, rejected and feel unloved. Well, duh — the people "dissing" us are on assignment to show us how we treat ourselves! They say we teach people how to treat us by the way we treat ourselves. What type of treatment are YOU teaching?

Recovering from addiction

Perhaps you aren't a former addict, but you're close to someone who is. In order to help someone in recovery — whether it's recovery from substance abuse, or mental and emotional self-abuse — you must educate yourself about their addiction. You must find out what their triggers are and learn to support them so that they will not become recidivism casualties.

Here are signs that showed me that I suffered from feelings of being enough:

- Craving attention from others

- Seeking recognition and affirmation from others

- Obsession with social media likes

Do you notice something? Everything I sought was external. I'd assumed I had nothing within me to draw from. Everything I desired, everything I needed, was within me. I just didn't know how to access it.

I realize now that one of the reasons we cannot change our thinking is because we don't *think* first; we *feel* first. Let's face it... At times, we can be emotionally led — not thinking first. If we thought first about the entire picture instead of letting our emotions lead us and cause us to act first, we would get the outcome that we so desire. Our thoughts create feelings, those feelings create emotions, and those emotions create belief, which causes us to act.

Because I was emotionally driven, I made a lot of poor decisions. My emotions had been in the driver's seat and my thoughts in the back seat. It wasn't until the effect of those emotions cost me my identity that I began to think. I began to do soulwork.

Soulwork is something we all must do as individuals. Soulwork involves identifying our triggers — the emotions that cause us to quit taking care of ourselves, and the subconscious hurt to which this behavior is attached. In order to create a different life, we must detach ourselves from the life we no longer want.

Tell yourself the truth. Ask yourself the tough questions. Look within as you finish these sentences:

It hurts me when _____.
I feel unloved when _____.
I feel unaccepted when _____.
I feel worthless and not good enough when _____.
I feel like I have no value when _____.

Then, affirm yourself daily:

I feel loved when _____.
I feel happy when _____.
I feel accepted when _____.
I feel good about pursuing my goals and dreams when _____.
I feel valuable when _____.

These are just a few examples of how to look at your life and identify your addiction triggers — the things that prompt you to become offended by other people's actions and go into defensiveness mode. Once you identify the root cause of your addiction, you can work on digging that root up so that new seeds of truth can be planted.

Self-Acceptance

So, I'm back in the court of my mind, and the prosecuting attorney is being a real piece of work. My opening argument today is centered on acceptance of who I am, an identity that differs drastically from how people have me pegged. The mask I had worn from birth had been suffocating me, preventing the real me from surfacing. I had built walls that I had designed to protect me. The prosecuting attorney contended that these were not walls, but rather my twisted attitude; that it was I who created this mountain of mess and was to blame for all the wrongs in my life.

I wait for the Judge to overrule the prosecutor, but He doesn't. I am starting to think I have no hope of winning this courtroom battle. I feel powerless. The faceless crowd sits motionless, listening as the prosecutor cuts me to pieces. I collect myself and ask for a short recess. It's granted: two hours.

***

My preliminary hearing in Detroit has also gone into recess. I step out of the courtroom wearing a black dress from one of my favorite stores. The dress has a fitted bust, an Empire waist and voluminous skirt. I've accented it with a single-strand pearl necklace.

Marco is waiting for me in the main lobby. As we leave the courthouse, he asks how the hearing has gone so far. I break down in tears because it has not gone well for me. He reminds me of all the past struggles I suffered and assures me that justice will prevail.

"Babe, what did I tell you that you needed to do? Keep sharing and speaking until you are heard," he says.

His voice is soothing and calming. My tears soon go away. I even manage to crack a smile ... a halfhearted smile, but a smile nonetheless.

"That's my Queen!" Marco exclaims "You've got the power in you, so go back in there and show 'em what you got! You're a fighter, not a quitter!" ♦

He is right. I have not traveled this far to give up. I must get myself together, go back into the courtroom that afternoon, and keep plugging.

We have some time to kill before the hearing reconvenes, so we decide to head to a restaurant for a bite to eat. I love corned beef, so we locate a spot on Congress Street that serves it.

As we begin to walk down Congress I look back at the courthouse, still wondering whether coming here to defend myself in this case was worth the time. I catch sight of the monument in front of the building, which is attracting quite a bit of attention. A forearm extends from the large, oblique structure. In the hand is a bronze gavel, held upright. This gavel is a symbol of justice.

We get to the restaurant and settle in. My spirits try to take another dip. Despite the encouragement from my earthly king, I still feel somewhat defeated.

As I continue to process the case in my mind, it and the case going on in the court of my mind become one. I think about the mental walls I'd created to protect me from my greatest fears. In my attempt to keep out the pain, I had inadvertently locked it in, and because I didn't know, love, or accept myself, I placed blame. I blamed those who'd mistreated me. But I'd never dealt with ME because I didn't know me.

"Babe... why do I feel that my mask has suffocated me, and there is no way to allow the truth of me to get out?" I ask, referring to my mental struggle. "I feel I need to suffocate the true me — to exchange the cultivation and growth of the true me for the counterfeit. How do I free myself and break the walls I created?"

"Stop worrying yourself," Marco replies. "I told you over and over — just speak. It'll all come together; trust me!"

I enjoy a nice corned beef sandwich and a plate of romaine salad with bright orange cherry tomatoes, croutons, feta cheese, and bacon bits, drizzled with a hint of ranch dressing. Marco has a turkey club made with Boars Head Honey Glazed Turkey, bacon, lettuce, two slices of bold, bright beefsteak tomatoes and mayonnaise. We take in the downtown-Detroit sights and enjoy the views as well as each other. It's nice to be home. But I can't wait to get back to my life, my True Self.

My husband looks at his watch. "Time to get back on the stand, Babe," he announces. "Let's wrap it up." He looks at me and, in a stern voice, asks. "What did I tell you to remember to do?"

I smirk back at him. "I know, I know... Just go in there and tell my story until I am heard. I got it, I hear you, and I love you."

Marco then plants a wet kiss on me. As I turn to walk away, he gives me a pat on the rear and says, "You got this!"

I giggle like a high-school girl, feeling so in love with this man and thanking GOD for bringing us together again.

***

For too long I'd hidden behind a mask that had allowed me to avoid dealing with the true me — a little girl whose development had been arrested due to lack of exposure and a traumatic past. My reality was based on my experiences and I'd told myself so many lies, I'd begun to believe them. The seed of love was never watered; the seeds of lies were what I continued to cultivate, grew and harvest. And this was a harvest I no longer desired.

If I was ever going to find the truth of who I was and realize my purpose, I would have to dig through the lies and get all the way to the root so new seeds could be planted and I could experience the life I truly desired. I had a lot of digging to do. My voice had been silenced during childhood. My story was never told because my identity had been hidden from me, by me, to protect me from my greatest enemy ... me. The saddest part of this truth is that these seeds of internal dysfunction were unknowingly passed down from generation to generation, from unconscious parents to children likewise born into a residual state of unconsciousness. For me to offer my children something different and break this cycle, I had to WAKE UP and acknowledge the existence of the cycle.

And in this truth, I also had to come full circle and learn how to break up with pieces of myself, pieces that harbored toxic emotions tied to my past. I once read an online article, "Self-esteem: Why do I look at myself in the mirror all the time?" by Fabienne Broucaret at Maria France Asia, the sister website for *Marie* magazine (mariefranceasia.com). In a nutshell, Broucaret wrote that if you have allowed your mirror to become the source of validation of your value, it is because you do not feel at ease when you receive gratitude, congratulations, and words of encouragement. Broucaret urged readers to "get rid of this embarrassment by simply learning to accept compliments, without trying to read between the lines, without asking what they hide, without minimizing them and without protesting by saying that you do not deserve them." The article hit home with me. This practice is one of the pieces of me that I had to break up with as I asked myself, "Who am I? No, really — who AM I?"

Now *knowing* who I am, I have decided not to be a slave to fear, insecurity, doubt or self-hate. I decided that I will no longer carry the generational curse that has been perpetuated, the family curse passed down to the unconscious seeds in the womb. I will no longer pretend not to know my predestined, preordained right to greatness before the foundation of this world. GOD has already prepared for ME a life as a CONSCIOUS WOMAN.

I once heard a pastor say, "We can't be governed by what seems right by others." In other words, he was saying, "Don't let other people's perception about you change you." For many years, I tried to live a life governed by others who surrounded me with false love. I would hear someone tell me, "Love you," without recognizing that this was not true love. My mother's love was not expressed with words, but with tangible items ... clothes, shoes, food on the table and a roof over my head. Momma did not know any other way to love me, because she herself did not understand what love meant. Scripture teaches us that "love is patient, love is kind. It does not envy, it does not boast, it is not proud" (I Cor. 13:4, NIV). Blessedly, I was taught about love by GOD. I am finding my way as I walk with GOD and let Him show me how to embrace the most excellent way of love.

Chapter Six
I Choose ME

These days, when you upgrade your smartphone, you may find that the new phone comes with many features with which you're unfamiliar. You may be one of those people who is reluctant to read the instructions that come with a new product. I, for one, am wired in a way that I like to try to figure things out on my own. (Just as I balk at reading the instructions on how to use a new phone and all its fancy bells and whistles, I balk at others trying to run my life.)

But when it comes to that upgrade, you don't really have a choice in the matter. You need to read the instructions and carefully learn all those new features. If you don't, chances are you will program your phone all wrong. You don't want to do that, do you?

Life's upgrades come with an abundance of instructions. The instruction manuals come in such forms as self-improvement and self-help books, including the Bible itself; conferences; workshops and webinars. Among the most common upgrade tools for women are conferences and seminars geared specifically toward them. At these events, women leaders serve as role models and use Bible/Christian book studies to help participants empower themselves.

It's up to you to choose to study these manuals and make the necessary applications. There are things you must put into place to begin to understand this thing called life. And, you must position yourself around people who understand your journey. As you read the instructions to your upgrade, you will probably gravitate toward those who have had similar walks and who also want an upgrade, but are not quite certain how to obtain one.

It is vitally important to educate yourself on what upgrading, or elevating, yourself in life entails. When you upgrade it is, in essence, an opportunity to liberate yourself: "I can operate this way. I can do this."

Some think that upgrading is an overnight process, but it doesn't work that way. You have to build character. I needed to build my character. I needed to develop integrity and self-control, because I'd never walked in either in my early life. I had the features that made an upgrade possible, but did not understand them. Nor did I have the right "software" in the form of mental makeup or cognitive ability. I was wired all wrong, running the wrong program. But with time, after reading the instructions correctly — taking a step back and self-reflecting — I was able to better understand myself.

I then realized that the features making one's upgrade possible are connected to many other power sources. My power sources are my husband, children and grandchildren. They are the parts on the circuit board that connect me, ground me and complete me. I had spent so much time giving, giving, giving myself to other people, I'd forgotten about taking care of myself. Half the time there was nothing *left* for me. I was like a smartphone that had been put up without being plugged into a charger and whose battery had, as a result, been drained of its power. I had to figure out a better scenario, because the one that had played out in my life had become old and tired! I had to not only upgrade; I had to ensure that the things that were important to me would be in that upgrade. The old version of me was disconnected; anything that had been attached to it was virtually wiped out. The only thing I took from the old me was the subscriber identity module, or SIM card, consisting of my higher self — which was always present – and my immediate family.

After writing out my legal brief for my appearance in the court of my mind, I realized just how refreshing my upgrade was. I tried to understand why, all this time, I had been unable to find the programs I was able to activate with the upgrade. Well … that was simple. For the first time, there was *space* for those programs. Praise GOD, won't He do it! But it took me many tries to figure this out. And it wasn't until I decided I needed to take the stand in that mental court when all things came to fruition. For first time in a long time, I had good reception. Things were beginning to become clear.

So, I went on to choose *me* over *them* ... those others to whom I had once given so much and who'd brought no added value into my life. My attitude was, *I support you, love you, but I think I'm gonna rock it out over here and not over there with you. Deal with that.* I chose to upgrade on my own and pay *my* bill, not theirs, and as a result my "relationships" with these people were disconnected. They weren't happy, but that no longer mattered because I felt so much better about myself.

I had to power up, get charged up. I had to start connecting with the right people in order to stay powered up and resourceful to myself. Had I stayed at that lower self and undergone no upgrade, I ultimately would have become powerless ... my battery life would have been depleted.

When you upgrade and power up, you then are connected to a greater source that leads you to life more abundant.

Real Me vs. Other Me

My old decisions had caused me to sacrifice myself for the sake of others in order to feel loved and accepted. But this had created my capacity to love past what I saw, felt, heard, or believed. I realized that the battle I'd been fighting was one for which I'd had no training, and no equipment had been provided. Yet I chose to get in the ring and use what I'd learned to win this battle, a battle called generational curses. No one talks about their issues; everyone hides. So, I had no idea what I might be hit with or how many times I might get hit. Yet I kept showing up, because I knew the person I'd become was not who I was created to be.

I knew I had to fight for the true me to manifest. The hits from the curse were intense, and hard to deal with, because they were internal. I couldn't see them, yet I felt them. I'd taken so many blows, never realizing that I was internally bleeding. And because all things are spirit first, the bleeding I was experiencing internally came to be displayed externally — financially, spiritually, physically and emotionally. The pressures of this life had caused me to run, because I couldn't bear any more pain. But, since running would never change what was happening inside me, I had to quit and face the pressure so that the bleeding could stop. That is the way you stop a hemorrhage, right? Apply pressure.

I quit running once I became aware of my patterns. I had to keep fighting. But this time I knew what I was fighting. I was fighting me, which gave me insight on how I needed to get back in the ring. I had more confidence this time that I could win. This thing, this giant, had to come on the scene, but I would be the one to make it fall. The giant had multiple facets … unworthiness, abandonment, rejection, insecurity. I had been under attack since before I was born. I was created in the image/spirit likeness of GOD, but my parents' passed-on generational curses smothered that truth.

For me to be who GOD created me to be, I had to fight to become her. By the time I became aware of who He created me to be, I was tired of fighting and just wanted to lie down and die. That was because I had come to the end of myself, my flesh. But then that I remembered the scripture: "'Not by might nor by power, but by my Spirit,' says the LORD Almighty" (Zechariah 4:6, NIV). I thought I had to fight physically, but this wasn't a physical fight. The greater One within me said, "You can't die, and neither can you lie down. When you get tired in your physical body, doing what you've always done, then the Spirit can take the wheel and lead you into victory. This fight is not physical; it's spiritual."

I knew that once I won this spiritual battle in my mind, I'd have won them all.

Rules of engagement

As I begin to remove the mask I've been hiding behind, it's important for me to understand how I got to this place, and a must-do as I move into that bleak boxed space, the courtroom of my mind. I need to know as much as I can fit into my head as I prepare to step before the jury, my accusers, who will determine my fate.

As a little girl, I remember wanting to have someone to talk to. There's nothing wrong with that; the desire to connect, and form relationships with others, is innate. But ... Momma worked long hours and was not demonstrative. Nurturing a child is a significant element in the human-development experience. An article at the website PsychCentral.com, "Mother-Son Relationship Important for Emotional Growth," cites a study by researchers at the School of Psychology and Clinical Language Sciences, University of Reading. The study revealed that "a mother's relationship with her children during youth is important for the child's emotional growth," according to the article. The relationship I longed to have with my mother was not there. And there was no one else to talk to; my brother had a life of his own and I had very few friends. So I often found myself pretending. I wanted to become somebody else. I told myself I was not good enough. *They don't like me. I'm not pretty enough. My feet are too big,* I concluded. One's childhood is supposed to be filled with happy, wonderful experiences. "Who told you that great lie?" that other self was shouting in my ear.

It *must* have been a lie, I concluded. After all, when I told my mother about being molested by Joe, she did not shake or thunder with rage as a protective lioness does when her cubs are threatened. It was many years before I found out her painful secret ... one of those generational curses from which sufferers never seem to be able to shake themselves free; one of those dark family secrets our elders dismiss by saying, "What goes on behind closed doors, stays behind closed doors!" People who make this statement have no clue how twisted this way of thinking is or how damaging it can be — well in my case, how damaging it *was*. My mother did not protect me and this vile creature, her boyfriend, stole my innocence and my voice from me. My childhood was ripped away in an instant. So, I began to question myself — *Was I wrong to perceive what I knew was wrong in my spirit? Was I to blame? Was it something I said, something I wore, or just my youth and freshness that caused this unwanted attention?* It had to be.

This situation took on another face as I matured physically. Since there was no love or affection that served as the foundation of our mother-daughter relationship, I began to spiral into self-destructive behavior. I was, as they say, a hot mess! I know it is not nice to speak ill of any vessel GOD created, but I was mistreating the TEMPLE He created: my body. I did not give two rats' you-know-whats about the things I was doing to it. Nor did I care what would run across it and to it.

It was only in recent years that I came to understand the patterns of my self-destruction. And it was only in recent conversations that I learned that my mother was also a silent victim. Given that, I had to make peace with her and forgive her. I had a great deal of soul searching to do, as well as a lot of healing. And I had to get myself ready to face the biggest battle of my life. I had to prepare to stand and defend myself — "claim my Adult Me, and LOVE Me until the last days I stand!"

I started reading articles online and becoming more insightful as I prepared to face the jury, to plead my case, in the court of my mind. I learned that, as the study mentioned above indicated, children naturally thrive when connected closely to their parents. This relational connection echoes the unborn baby's physical connection to the mother via the umbilical cord — the lifeline of a baby before his or her debut. A child's tendency to seek connection to the mother by whom that child was nurtured in the womb explains why children are seemingly "hardwired to become attached to caretakers," according to an online fact sheet on abandonment and attachment-related trauma (and its treatment) for The Refuge — A Healing Place, a national treatment center for those suffering from post-traumatic stress disorder, trauma, depression, addictions and co-occurring disorders.

As I started to read articles on abandonment and attachment and started to examine my own life, I began to realize that what happened to me was not my fault ... even though others have had me labeled "guilty as charged."

The memories that flood my mind are painful. I go right back to that thing called LOVE ... something I craved so deeply. I'd battled daily to find peace and solace with my past, trying to do as they do in the business world — write it off. Unfortunately, this kind of pain has a lingering effect. It nearly destroyed me. I tried to leave this dark place, but kept coming back to that thought: *My mom just let it happen.*

She did not "let it happen." She simply did not know how to respond. When I told her what was going on, she saw the mirror image of herself in me. She was too terrified to utter a word in my defense. And at that moment, through her silence, I lost my voice.

Now, the more I read, the more I learn, and the more I learn, the better I understand myself. No longer am I sad. I can face my accusers and stand proud, strong and whole. I don't care what anyone might think or say, because my Judge already knows my truth. So, I walk in and take the stand in the court of my mind, knowing that no jury can break me.

For each witness who steps out of the darkness to give testimony, my Defense Attorney — also GOD — has armed me with knowledge. In this movement of self-discovery, self-improvement, self-love and strengthened self-esteem, I have learned to love myself and not be ashamed.

Naked and Not Ashamed

According to the online Merriam-Webster Dictionary, "uncover" means:
— to remove a cover from (something)
— to find or become aware of (something that was hidden or secret)
— to allow (something) to be seen by removing a covering

GOD tells us in 2nd Corinthians 4:7 that there is treasure — the gospel and its truths — in earthen vessels. For me to find my treasure, I had to uncover all the lies behind which I had been hiding.

Being naked and not ashamed is all about uncovering the things our parents, society, religion, etc., has taught us to hide. As long as it's hidden, it carries guilt and shame and has power over you. Once you become naked and not ashamed, you take your power back.

My journey started about 10 years ago when I began asking myself some tough questions: *Are you happy? Why do you keep letting people use you? Why don't you desire your husband anymore? Why are you deceiving yourself? Why don't you believe you're enough?*

Answering these questions was going to require me to do something different, which meant I had to face my fears. I began the journey to seek out the truth of why I did what I did. I realized that I was numb. As an adult, I hadn't allowed myself to be vulnerable because of the lie I'd told myself, the lie that I had to be the strong one. Where did I get that lie from? By taking on the responsibility of being the strong one, I disconnected from my emotional self and became what everyone else needed and wanted me to be. That meant that I no longer mattered. I self-sacrificed and chose to quit feeling.

I was at home by myself one day when I discovered this truth. I *knew* I had a serious problem when, despite the fact that no one was home with me, I still refused to cry! *What is wrong with me?* I asked myself. I sat there in disbelief, realizing that no one had ever told me that it was OK to express one's feelings. As a matter of fact, I had never seen my mother shed a tear. She'd never showed any emotion, so neither did I.

I knew I needed to cry, so that day, home alone, I gave myself permission to feel. It felt awkward at first, so I shut my feelings off again. This is when I realized that I had *control* over my feelings and emotions — I could turn them on and I could turn them off. I sat there on the edge of my bed, hurting on the inside, wanting to be free from the pain. But I continued to hold it like a mother nurturing a baby.

I sat there a little longer, then I was led to wrap my arms around myself and say, "It's OK. Let it go." Then I began to cry like a baby! I held myself and rocked and rocked until I felt a sense of relief. As much as I wanted to experience something different, it was never going to happen until I told myself it was OK.

We have the power within us to change every situation, and if you're like I once was, you probably have no clue as to how to access it.

One day, shortly after I'd shed my numbness and had that first healing cry, I was walking through a local department store when a flood of emotions came out of nowhere. I began to cry again! I immediately ran to my car because I was still ashamed to show emotion and didn't want anyone to see me that way. What was I hiding from? What was I covering up and why? I was hiding from the truth that my life experiences had hurt me, damaged me and left me broken. Because I thought the things I'd experienced were my fault, I hid myself, harboring fear, guilt and shame. I didn't want to keep living this way, and I had to make some serious decisions. I had to face the accuser, the enemy ("in-a-me") within. I had to uncover those lies — because who keeps a treasure hidden? I wanted my treasure to be uncovered so that I could share it with the world.

The only way to uncover that treasure was to seek so that I could find. Seeking would require me to take the less traveled road … the narrow road.

Chapter Seven
Delivered ... AND Set Free

I've been approached by a number of women who have been molested and wanted to talk about it. It made me realize that there are so many others suffering in silence ... frightened, guilty and ashamed. What I tell them — and what I want all victims of sexual abuse to know — is that what happened to them wasn't their fault.

My passion is helping women to identify and face their trauma and thereby become freed from it. I think the reason so many of us remain victims of our trauma is because we are resistant to being freed. If you are a survivor of a traumatic experience such as the one I suffered, how is that trauma playing out in various parts of your life today?

I remember Marco once asking me what I enjoyed about our intimacy. I thought about it, and realized that I couldn't tell him. Because of what I'd suffered all those years ago, I had not made an intimate connection with anybody. I'd closed that part of myself off. GOD intended for intimacy to take place between married couples. Intimacy does include sexual intercourse, but, according to the first definition listed at Dictionary.com, it's also "a close, familiar, and usually affectionate or loving personal relationship with another person." Within a marriage, both definitions should apply. But, I realized, I was just going through the physical motions. Why? Because the part of me that was supposed to be engaging in that *first* definition of intimacy was closed off. It's like having a baby. When that seed is planted, the brain automatically does what it's supposed to do for the body to respond and the seed to grow. We don't tell it to grow. It was the same thing with me. That trauma, that seed, that mindset of *I've got to protect myself and I can't let anybody in this area,* had grown and had kept me from fully engaging in my marriage.

And there is such a thing as being delivered from something, but not set free from it.

I was *delivered* from molestation at Joe's hands, but I was not set free. My trauma played out in looking for love in all the wrong places, using all the wrong methods. I had that same record playing in my head, over and over: *Momma didn't love me. Momma didn't accept me. Momma chose a man over me.* I didn't experience peace, love and acceptance as a child. So, my life became a journey in which I tried to find what I was supposed to have gotten in my first home. Not only did I look for love in all the wrong places, I was ill-equipped to enjoy real intimacy found in the right places.

Speaking of homes, another sign that I still needed to be set free was my initial attitude about the palatial country home with which GOD blessed my family and me some years ago. There's a crude but true saying that goes like this, and please excuse my French: You can't turn a "ho" into a housewife. What that saying conveys is that you can put a loose woman in a traditional family situation, but if she still has those loose-woman tendencies, she will continue to be who she is. Because of my mental struggle, my mind remained in not-good-enough mode when it came to ownership of this phenomenal home. Physically I was there, but mentally I wasn't. Delivered, but not set free!

The best way to be freed from our trauma is to face it ... mentally and/or physically. We so often run from our fears, run from our pain, then suffer as a result. In my mother's case, even when she got to a point where she could talk about her molestation, her subconscious continued to deny that it happened. For her, being freed meant going back to the actual location where the trauma took place. The mental roadblock she'd put up was the reason she had been unable to attract a man with whom she could enjoy a healthy relationship. (Since being set free, she has had men flock to her like crazy! Her energy has shifted and that has opened new possibilities for her.)

As I'd stated previously, I was programmed to stay loyal to dysfunction, so I maintained a relationship with my momma despite her having denied my molestation and having chosen to stay with Joe. We went through years and years and years of doing just what needed to be done to get by. We stayed in close proximity with each other; I moved to Arkansas, her homeland, in 2003 to be near her after my father passed away. I was able to convince myself that our relationship was OK, because this is what I'd learned to do. And I thought I had forgiven her. But the baggage remained.

In 2015 my mother, who lives with us, had surgery. As she recovered, Marco and I took care of her. Marco was the one who gave her the attention she'd longed for from a man. "Momma, what you need?" he'd ask. She ate it up.

One evening, I was tired from working one of the 16-hour days I sometimes put in as an entrepreneur. Needing to be attended to, my mother called me: "Chris, come here."

"No baby, you lay down; I'll get her," Marco said before I could get up.

"OK," I replied. He went to see about her.

About 20 minutes later, my mother called me again. This time, I got up and went into her bedroom … and found her in an irritable mood. "When I call you, I need you to come and see what it is that I want," she fussed. "I wouldn't have called you if I didn't need you."

Instantly, something went over me. The thought pushed through my subconscious: *But when I needed you, you didn't come to see about me. So now here you are, lying on your back, and you need me to come to see about you.*

At that moment I heard the HOLY SPIRIT say, "Give her what she was unable to give you." I could have let bitterness overtake me and said "No." But I didn't. I obeyed GOD.

I also had to face the realization that the attention Momma gave my husband, in response to his attention, had made me a bit resentful. As a child I'd felt she'd given my brother, as well as Joe, more attention than she did me. *Well, here she is again, choosing a man over me,* I thought.

This experience showed me what I had yet to overcome. GOD was giving me the opportunity to make a turning point for the better.

A couple days or so after this interchange, GOD spoke to me again about my mother.

"She needs to know that you've forgiven her," He said.

"She knows that I've forgiven her. We live together," I protested.

"No, she's still carrying that guilt," GOD said.

I realized this was true. My mother naturally likes to stay busy; she has a servant's heart. But she stayed extra-busy around our house. I realized that, in going so hard for me, she was trying to overcompensate for not being there for me during my childhood.

So I again obeyed GOD.

"Momma, you don't owe me anything," I told her. I appreciate everything you do for me, but you don't owe me anything. All you owe me is love. You did the best you could with what you had. You don't have to do all this stuff."

And it was during this conversation that she broke down and released that burden she'd been carrying,

I think of all those years she must have beat herself up, asking herself, *Why didn't I listen to her? Why didn't I hear her? Why didn't I protect her?* I'm surprised, and grateful, that she didn't end up in a mental institution.

In the court of my mind I was vindicated by the Judge ... my GOD. Not the people. He helped me to see that I was vindicated. I had lived in a prison of subconscious thinking, not taking the time to identify why I did what I did. We as a people tend to repeatedly play out the same stories of our lives. With my mom, I had the opportunity to change the course and play out what I would have experienced had she heard me all those years ago; has she not forced me to stay quiet and had I not gone on to replay the cycle of my trauma into my adult life.

The way I lost my voice is very important because it goes back to the ways we traditionally raised our children. If you were raised in an old-school home, you were probably told to speak only when being spoken to ... to stay quiet when grown folks are talking ... and to *never* question authority. Even within the church, you are all too often persecuted if you question authority. Imagine that; the very place you're supposed to be free turns out to be yet another prison. So you're in prison in your home, then you're supposed to go to the church and get free, but you end up pushed into a deeper pit and you think, *I don't know WHAT I'm supposed to be doing or how to get free.*

The journey back to you begins, first and foremost, with your realization of what GOD created us to be. He created us to be love! *We are love.* We are looking outside ourselves for what is already in us. We just haven't been taught that it's there. We've been looking for GOD outside of us, but He is within us. He said He would never leave us nor forsake us (Deut. 31: 6; Hebrews 13:5). We quote this line of Scripture without realizing we have forsaken ourselves. We're running from the truth of *who* GOD created us to be and *what* lies inside of us, and it's because nobody's showed us. Therefore, we look for fulfillment in alcohol; we look for it in partying; we look for it in drugs; we look for it in sex. We look for it in all these different places and fail to find it. Until you find out who you really are, you don't find your tribe. The Trinity — the Father, Son and Holy Ghost – are all within you. But if you aren't taught this, and if love wasn't shown within your original home, you don't realize it's within you. Again, you look for it outside yourself. When you look at society, you see myriad people in search of what has lived in them all along, unaware that GOD has created in all of us everything we need.

Everyone yearns to be accepted and loved. I believe that when you accept CHRIST, you are accepting yourself. You and He are already one. In Matthew 22:37-39, JESUS says: "'You must love the Lord your GOD with all your heart, all your soul, and all your mind.' This is the first and greatest commandment. A second is equally important: 'Love your neighbor as yourself.'" (NLT). If He wasn't talking about you in the first verse, why would He then say in the second, 'Love your neighbor as yourself"? He was saying to love YOU (you who are one with GOD) with your heart, soul and mind, then love your neighbor as yourself. Until we love our neighbors as ourselves, we will continue to experience division and separation in the world.

And in order to really find your tribe, or find where you belong, you've got to find *you*. That's what JESUS was saying in Matthew 6:33: "Seek ye first the kingdom of GOD" (KJV) ... seek who you are in Him, rather than looking to others for validation and acceptance. Our experiences in our first physical home come through our early experiences with our parents, through which we usually have our first experience with GOD. But nine times out of 10, the father isn't in the home, and Momma's got "man issues." Such experiences teach us to reject what is in us ... and that self-rejection can play out in every part of our lives.

I looked for love and acceptance in many places because I did not find it in my first home. Not that my mother didn't love me. But she was trying to heal from what she herself didn't get as a child. She was trying to love me from a place of her own lack. As parents, we are affected by the unmet needs we had as children. We then fail to give our children what they need.

So where did that leave me, a child growing up in a home where the mother didn't get what she needed? Rejected and abandoned. Why? Because my mother couldn't give me what she didn't have. So many people are angry at their mothers and fathers because of what they didn't get from them. But if the parents themselves weren't exposed to those things, how could they give them to their children?

I've said a lot about loving and accepting ourselves; I also want to point out the importance of accepting people where they are. We tend to want to force others to be like us or see things our way, but everybody has his or her own personal experience. The other person's lens is different from our lens. Remember my saying earlier that I was trying to *show* others how to love me because I was scared that if I *told* them, they wouldn't hear me?

Having not had my life experience, these others were unable to read my sign language. So, my efforts did not work. All I did was encounter more rejection and abandonment. There I was, trying to show people how to love me and they, of course, didn't get it.

As I stated before, I went so far as to look for a mother figure within the church ... look for a momma in other women, trying to satisfy my personal and emotional needs. Same deal: Those who didn't know my life experience couldn't give me what I needed.

Because we expect others to see things the way we do, we are offended by their decisions. And it's causing more division. The reason we can't love and accept others as they are is because we can't love and accept *ourselves* as *we* are. We struggle to be in control of how we think and how we see things. And we reach out and try to control others.

Again, I must mention the traditional church, where they try to make us act a certain way and do certain things to be accepted. As a member of a traditional-church body, I was so aggravated because I felt I couldn't be me. I'm silly. I like to have fun. I'm just a clown! But in the church, I had to be reserved. I couldn't do this; I couldn't do that.

To be able to identify why we do what we do is key. If we don't ever ask ourselves those questions, we've just accepted second best. And here's the messed-up part: When things come easily, we think there's something wrong. In our minds, everything *has* to be complicated in order to be true. Because our lives have been so complex, we think there must be an ulterior motive when someone chooses to love us or be a blessing to us.

I once struggled with that issue when it came to my husband. Marco loves me so freely and unconditionally. He will do anything for me. But occasionally the thought crossed my mind: *This is fake. He will show his true colors in a while. Who puts up with a broken woman who's dealt with all kinds of men, and attacked his ego and self-esteem by saying negative things to him? Who does that?*

GOD had to tell me, "This is Me in the flesh, walking with you as your husband. I'm not going to take My love from you. I'm going to remain steadfast and unmovable." And He has. The Bible tells us that the Word became flesh and dwelt among men. My husband is the perfect example of the living Word becoming flesh and dwelling among men ... so that I could experience Him.

However, I came to a point where I had to acknowledge that I was sabotaging my marriage. I subconsciously hated men and had no respect for them because of the men who had been part of my life:

My father

My father wasn't present in my life. He was not a part of my physical home because my parents divorced when I was a baby.

He made promises to me (i.e., promises to come and get me so that we'd spend time together) and didn't keep them. He chose a woman over me.

Joe, my mother's boyfriend

Joe was a man I grew to trust because he was in the home. But when I was 12, he molested me, took my innocence, then made me feel like I was wrong for using my voice and telling the truth.

My second son's father

This man turned out to be a cheater. He didn't value me and had no respect for me at all. He not only took advantage of my heart; he took from me, period.

Ralph, my ex-husband

A single mother of two at the time, I married Ralph because I didn't want my sons to grow up without a father. I wanted them to have a man within the home. But I didn't realize I was causing more damage than good. I stayed loyal to my dysfunction. Ralph and I were drawn to each other because of our brokenness; we wore the titles of husband and wife, but in reality, we grew up together. We were two kids, raising kids. During our 17-year journey, I started reading and finding myself. I encouraged Ralph to do the same, but he refused. He was comfortable being him and because he chose himself and not me, I resented him and stayed angry at him for quite some time. I wanted to control his decision making, but that was not for me to do. We all are free to choose for ourselves. I had to accept Ralph's decision, and I had to stand in my truth.

My sons

My two eldest sons grew up and chose to live a life away from me. Silently, I was hurt at their leaving me, but I never expressed it; I didn't feel the need to do so. I had assumed they would stay close to me because they were grateful for the sacrifices I'd made to be the best possible mother to them.

My brother

My brother was a father figure in that he provided for me, took care of me and hung out with me, but then he left me to live a life of his own

Marco, my husband and real "Mr. Right"

Marco showed up and gave me my heart's desire. But the previous men in my life had hurt me sooooo badly, I didn't believe he wouldn't end up doing as they'd done. Although he was physically in the house with me, I wouldn't admit him to my inner home. I kept him on the front porch of that home, which was full of hurt. I guess that's why I still struggle with accepting parts of myself. But, thank God, Marco's love remained consistent. I wanted badly to experience his love, but I didn't know how. I'm still learning how, in fact.

When you allow yourself to be vulnerable, you open yourself up to be watered for growth. Now, when my husband speaks words of affirmation to me, I feel them. His words no longer land on stony ground; they land in my heart of flesh. I can now receive new seed into my heart to give birth to my heart's desire.

But at first, Marco's love was so foreign. To experience love without anything being required of them is a foreign thing to so many people.

The people we serve with our organization, True Self Ministries, are given this kind of love – love that does not require anything in return. For instance, one young woman, who is also one of my coaching clients, has lived with us for two years. She had some marital issues and needed a place to stay, so we provided that for her. When people see us, one of the things they say is, "I've never seen family operate like y'all operate. This is unreal. Y'all all get along. Y'all let people in that you don't know."

My reply is this: "What we do for people is a ministry. Ministry doesn't have to be happen within four walls of a church building."

For us to be game changers and world changers, we must be consistent in the lives of people. We must be determined to dig up that fallow ground, because it's hard. So many people have hearts that are hard — nothing can get in; nothing can get out. They're just existing. They look alive and awake, but they're really in that same comatose state I was in. It's not until we start facing truth that we wake up.

I can now experience life because I'm no longer living my mother's life; I'm living *my* life. I was intentional about finding out what my truth was, rather than living hers. Which is how you get free. Which is how you find your way back to you. Through True Self Ministries I love, and help to awaken, as many as GOD sends our way.

My mental court case consisted of me gathering all this evidence: My molestation. My marriage. My belief that I wasn't a good enough person or a good enough parent. All these thoughts – that's all they were, thoughts. Stinkin' thinkin' that had held me prisoner. In order for me to renew my thinking, I had to start asking myself the challenging questions, because a lot of that thinking was in my counterfeit DNA: My parents could only reproduce what they were. So, I was a product of my environment. My mother delivered me with everything she was, so I had to find out who I was. In order for me to be set free, I had to take the journey myself.

Chapter Eight
A Degree of Success

Just as I was found innocent in the court of my mind, I was found innocent in my literal court case. I was found innocent because I went back to the roots. Going back to the roots involved me going back to say, "OK, this happened and that happened." We *choose* to forget what we don't *want* to remember, not realizing that our cells have memory. I had chosen to forget a whole lot of stuff. But I had to face the things I was running from if I was ever going to have a welcome-home experience and be able to live with my head and my heart in proper alignment. I had to go back and ask, "OK, who do they say I am?"

Based on what I'd heard from society, I was a fast-tail little girl who wasn't going to amount to anything. I was going to be another statistic. My kids were going to be in prison. These were word seeds. But I never received them. I was able to achieve a degree of success, having been externally motivated by everything everyone had said that I wouldn't be, or wouldn't do.

As I continued to struggle with my spiritual and mental identity theft, I built a work life that blossomed into entrepreneurship and marketplace ministry.

Marketplace ministry

I not only gave birth at the age of 15; I started my first job at that age, working at Foot Locker. I have worked ever since. I transitioned to entrepreneurship in 2006 when my then-husband and I opened a car-detailing business.

For me, business and ministry have long been intertwined somehow. Such was the case with a ministry GOD had directed us to leave. Sometimes, when GOD tells you to do something and you don't obey, He will allow situations and circumstances to push you out. We were pushed out of this ministry because we didn't leave when GOD told us to leave. After we left, those in the ministry badmouthed us viciously, claiming we had stolen from them. No one from the ministry would talk to us anymore.

I subsequently began going to Ambassador Brenda Jefferson's School of Ministry, through which I became an ordained minister. As it happened, the pastor of our former ministry taught one of the sessions for the school. I would get so aggravated at his presence.

One day the HOLY SPIRIT said, "When he gets finished teaching, go to him and apologize."

"GOD, he's the one going around talking about us! Why do I have to be the one to apologize?" I asked.

"It's not about you; it's about what I am doing through you, the HOLY SPIRIT replied. "Just do it."

I went and apologized to that pastor and his wife, even though I didn't feel I owed them an apology. But obedience is better than sacrifice. And, as a result, GOD went on to bless our car-detailing business tremendously.

This business came about despite some challenges that threatened its birth. After we transitioned to our new church, we began helping our pastor with his business. I was so excited about this ministry — the acceptance, the validation, the affirmation — that I felt I owed this pastor something. So, we ran his operation … for pennies. I don't know how we survived and ate, because we weren't getting paid much. Our pastor had promised to put a certain amount of money aside for us to branch off and start our own business after a certain time. When that time came, he produced an itemized list of things he said we owed him for and gave us almost no seed money for our business. It was a situation akin to the one in which black people in the post-slavery South served as sharecroppers, leasing land from white farmers who kept them indebted (and in bondage) by charging high interest rates on the credit they give the sharecroppers for farming supplies.

We subsequently borrowed money from a couple of other pastors to get the business going and managed to acquire everything we needed — except for one key item. The day before we were scheduled to open, we went into this gas station in Conway. "We are supposed to be starting our business tomorrow and we have cars lined up and we do not have a pressure washer," we told the man running the place, asking if he knew were we could get one.

To our amazement and delight, this man went into the back of his gas station, where he had a locked-up shed. He broke the lock off the door, went into the shed, came out with a pressure washer and gave it to us. Jehovah Jireh had provided! (My ex-husband operates this business to this day.)

I also ran a day care out of my home and, for a time, operated a beauty supply store in Morrilton, Ark. I was in cosmetology school and had a vision of a one-stop shop where people could come get their hair done, buy hair supplies and even purchase clothing. I had not been to business school, but I was a woman of faith and was not scared to jump out there. So, I jumped out there and leased this large building. My mom and I walked the streets of Morrilton in the morning, praying and calling in our confessions each day.

I found favor with the people in that town. I remember one gentleman — to this day I believe he was an angel — who came by while I was getting the building ready and told me, "I really admire your drive and your tenacity." Later, he asked me how much I needed to stock my store. I said I don't know. He asked if

I wanted a business partner. I didn't. "But if you want to invest, absolutely make an investment," I told him.

Unbeknownst to me, this man had been sharing my story with another gentleman. Two months or so later, the second gentleman walked into my store and handed me a check for $5,000. "Go stock your store," he said. "When I see the return from this investment, I'll give you another $5,000." I have not seen that man since. And, unfortunately, the store didn't survive as I had spread myself too thin. I was trying to finish school and put someone else in position to run the day care as well as start another business.

In addition to my entrepreneurial efforts, I worked with Choosing to Excel, a Conway-based nonprofit program begun in 1991 by Thelma Moton to help young people make positive life choices. Through this program, I went into middle, junior high and high schools not just in Conway, but around central Arkansas — Little Rock, Greenbrier and Morrilton — as well as the University of Central Arkansas at Conway and worked with girls to help them maintain high standards of conduct. I was hired because I had a passion for young girls, a passion that was connected to my trauma as a young girl. In talking to these girls and helping them, I was talking to and helping the little girl in me. I'd said I was called to teach these girls; in reality, they taught me. These girls had the courage to say the very things the little girl in me wanted to say, but didn't have the courage to say, all those years ago.

Helping them walk out their struggles helped me walk out of that little-girl archetype in which I'd been stuck.

The highlight of my time with the girls came during a summer camp, when we did an activity called Obituaries. During this activity, we buried our old selves, then did birth announcements for our new selves that were coming into the world. That camp was monumental for the girls and for me. I had 12 to 15 girls, age 12 and up. Each girl talked about who she *didn't* want to be, laid that person to rest, then stated who she *did* want to be. It was the most beautiful thing! The girls wept. And then we celebrated, because when you announce a birth, people celebrate. I had no idea that this activity with the girls was really for me: GOD was pouring out to me to pour out to them!

From there, passion for working with young girls grew. I became director of a program under the Choosing to Excel umbrella … G.E.M.S., or Girls Eagerly Maintaining High Standards. It was when working with G.E.M.S. that I realized I had a natural speaking gift. Even as a teenage mother, my desire had been to speak to other young girls. GOD was allowing me to live my dream!

My work with Choosing to Excel and G.E.M.S. laid the groundwork for True Self Ministries, the nonprofit Marco and I have launched to help people be who they were created to be. In addition to this ministry, we run a Medicaid transportation service for children with disabilities and those who need to get to their doctor's appointments, as well as an adult day care for the elderly. Scripture indicates that our latter years will be greater than our former years (Look at what GOD did for Job in the Old Testament!) so at the day care, we try to provide that experience. For instance, when the elderly develop physical or mental disabilities, they seldom get to go out to enjoy themselves. We create a going-out experience, complete with formal dining, for our clients – and they love it.

My husband and I have also started a travel business that ties into True Self and is geared toward women. As women, we work, we nurture, we take care of our husbands and children, we take care of the house. In all of that, we forget to do anything for ourselves. My desire is for women is to say "yes" to living again. In fact, the name of the travel company is Yes to Live. I plan to create trips, which may include one to two cruises a year, and take clients into an environment where they can be free and not worry about the cares of this world. That, to me, is the best opportunity to give people the truth. Clients will have workshops set up for them to learn how to birth their dreams into reality. They will also have a chance to receive personal coaching. I always think of how I can help people leverage their gifts. Not only will these trips benefit clients; they'll also benefit the speakers and coaches, who will have the opportunity to build their network and their following.

My mission is to expose people to new things on as grand a scale as I can manage. I know that without the exposure, one's desires never change. Ideally, exposing people to the best of possibilities will awaken something in them so that their desires will change for the better; so that mediocrity will no longer be acceptable to them and therefore, they will go after whatever they want. The only limits we have are the ones we place on ourselves.

I am thankful for all my accomplishments, but they did not come from an internal place. All my accomplishments were driven from a place of trying to prove to my accusers that I wasn't who they had contended I was. Their negative words were the driving force. I accomplished a lot; however, I never experienced or celebrated my accomplishments. I said I was doing it for me, and I was. But the motives behind my drive were from an emotional place. I was also trying to prove myself to people who couldn't care less about what or how I was doing.

Internally, my heart was closed, so actually *experiencing* success was a whole other matter. Earlier I mentioned that large, beautiful home GOD had blessed us with. At one point I realized I hadn't stopped to really *experience* the home – for instance, sit out in the yard or curl up in a corner and just be. If I was going to have internal freedom, I had to go back to where I was to reach the spiritual place where I am now, with head and heart in proper alignment. I had to face my Goliaths … my miscalibrated five senses, which were feeding contaminated information to my subconscious, which kept playing out that contaminated information. That led to my stinkin' thinkin', which is why I acted the way that I did. And then there was the matter of being emotionally led. It, along with my thinking, was part of the bad programming.

So I had to change my programming. I had to go back and say, "OK, this happened to me. But how do I see the good — and GOD — in this? What can I take away from this to impact to other people?" Sometimes we get so caught up in the trauma, we don't see the good that GOD can bring out of bad. I wouldn't be able to talk to other women who have been molested, for instance, had I not had the experience. So being able to say, "thank You, Lord," and maintain gratefulness even in what seems to be the worst moments, is key.

I returned to face my trauma with new eyes. *OK, this is how I perceived it*, I told myself. *But there's got to be some good in it. Let me go back and look at this thing again. They said I was a fast-tail girl, but that wasn't really the case; I was molested and exposed to sex at an early age, which caused me to continue to seek fulfillment through sex.*

Love is literally what saved, healed and delivered me. In addition to GOD's love, I benefited from the unconditional love of my husband and others close to me. I always say that relationships are vital. But until we get that relationship with ourselves straight, giving *us* what we need, we're going to be inconsistent in all our other relationships.

Speaking of relationships, you may be wondering by now whether I struggled in my early parenting before I made my journey back to me. The answer is YES! I didn't even realize I was struggling until I realized I was replaying my mother's story.

I always say I have two sets of kids. I say that because there's an 11-year gap between my three oldest and my two youngest. My eldest child — my 28-year-old son — was fathered by Marco from our first relationship, after which we went on our separate personal journeys to come back together. My second son is the result of another relationship. My ex-husband is the father of my daughter and my two youngest sons.

I feel that GOD gave me a second chance to do things differently with my youngest children.

One of the moments that highlighted this difference began with a conversation with my daughter when she 16 years old.

Let me lay some groundwork here: In addition to my having been taught to be loyal to dysfunction, another reason I stayed in bad relationships was because I didn't want my children to experience what I had experienced. I eventually realized that I'd done more damage than good. When I say that staying "for the sake of the children" is the worst thing you can do, believe me! Even though Ralph, my former husband, and I were growing apart, I stayed. My church taught that divorce was out of the question, no matter what; this also played a part in my staying put. I was even "prophesied to" by a minister who told me I couldn't leave. Already lacking knowledge of who I was, I listened to these voices.

As I'd mentioned, I ran a daycare business; my husband ran our detail shop, and I had my part-time job in the schools. Ralph struggled with financial stewardship, so I had to make up for his shortcomings in this area. My daughter saw me busting my rear end to help make ends meet for us. She saw me working all the time … and unhappy.

This conversation with her occurred one evening when she was in the kitchen, watching me work, and I'll never forget it.

"Momma, you're a good one," she said, leaning against the sink.

"What did you say?" I asked. "What do you mean, I'm a good one?"

"I couldn't do it," she said, clearly referring to all my butt-busting.

It was at that moment that I told myself, *Christel, you've got to do something. If not, she's going to do exactly what you've done — stay in an unhealthy relationship for the sake of keeping the family together and be miserable as a result.*

I'll be darned if my daughter didn't soon go on to do that very thing. She sacrificed all her goals and dreams for her first boyfriend. Don't be fooled; your kids aren't going to do as you *say*, they're going to do as you *do*. Their story may not look exactly like yours on the surface, but if you take a closer look, chances are you'll see them playing out your life, not their own. My daughter ran away to San Antonio to be with her boyfriend and ended up unhappy. She was afraid to admit this, however, until I reached out to her and said, "You don't have to live like that. You can come home if you need to." When she indicated that she wanted to come home, I drove to San Antonio and picked her up.

She'd followed the same path I had. I remember when she first came home with this young man, telling me about all they were doing. She was excited. But I noticed that she said nothing about the things she had once told me she wanted to do. She had been into modeling and dance. But she sacrificed these pursuits because her boyfriend was insecure and didn't want her in the limelight. She began to support him, even smoking weed just because he smoked weed. She was doing everything she could to make him happy. It was the same thing I had been doing – everything to make whatever man I was with happy while sacrificing my dreams, goals and desires.

I've got to do something different, I decided. *If I'm going to break this cycle, my daughter has got to* see *something different.* And she did. She saw me leave a marriage that simply was not working. She saw the progress I made when I started choosing *me.* I've received several affirmations from her — "Momma, thank you for breaking the cycle, for showing me how to find me, showing me how to love me, showing me how to be OK with me." She thanks me all the time because she saw that she was going down the same path.

With my two eldest sons, it was a different story. During their upbringing, they saw the broken, identity-robbed me. Because I — and he — didn't know who his father was for a time, my firstborn struggled with identity theft. His story reflected my story, but in a different way. He continues to struggle with who he is. My second oldest son is very aloof, very closed off. No surprise there; I didn't express myself, nor did my mother.

My desire to help them find themselves is such that I don't take offense when they get angry. I sent my eldest son a message once. "I know you're mad as hell at me," I wrote. "I *know* you are. And it's OK. Do whatever you have to do to free yourself of the thought that 'my momma screwed me up.' If you want to cuss, cuss. Cuss me out if you need to. I give you permission because I would be mad as hell too, to know that I didn't ask for this, that I was birthed into this, and now I'm struggling with it at 28."

"Momma, I would never disrespect you," he said.

"I understand that," I told him. "But I need you to understand that I understand your anger. I understand your frustration. I understand what you're dealing with. I love you and I want to hold your hand through it. I found my way back to me. And that's the only way I can help you find your way back to you."

There were some hurtful things I had to face. But I want to pass down generational blessings, not generational curses. And this kind of generational curse has been all too plentiful. There are many people who have never told their children that their father isn't who they thought their father was. Some people ask me, "Why did you tell?" I say that I wouldn't be able to live with myself if I allowed my son to walk around his entire life, not knowing who he was. This is too much of a societal struggle. Nobody knows who they are! Your momma didn't know who she was. Your daddy didn't know who he was. And since they didn't know who they were, you darn sure don't know who *you* are!

My three oldest children are now doing their soulwork. I'm able to walk them through it. Had I not done my soulwork, I wouldn't be able to help them.

Sometimes, we get frustrated when we witness the struggles our kids deal with. But we can learn from our children if we really take the time to listen. When we listen, we may well find out that their struggles are similar to ours. As parents, we don't want our kids to see us as not good enough. And I struggled, because what I'd heard as a 15-year-old was that I was not good enough. I fought hard against that perception others had of me then as that fast-tail girl who wasn't going to amount to anything and whose kids would end up in prison.

And I thank GOD that none of my children have gone to prison. When I moved from Detroit in 2003, I wanted to give them a better life. I didn't want them to grow up in the 'hood. So, we went from one extreme to another. Inner-city Detroit is all about drugs, sex, a whole lot of mayhem. They didn't like coming to Arkansas, but bringing them here, I believe, was the best thing.

As I tell people, parenting doesn't come with a handbook. It's the grace of GOD, and my love for my children, that got them this far. When I have conversations with them and they ask questions, I am very transparent with them about my struggles. Just by our conversations, my children have had major breakthroughs because they can see themselves. If parents talk to their kids about their struggles — rather than hide them because they're scared of being judged— they will see major breakthroughs in their lives as well.

They say your home is your first ministry. You can't minister to the home if you're hiding, so you've got to be naked and not ashamed. As Romans 8:1 indicates, there is no condemnation for those who are in CHRIST JESUS.

Chapter Nine
She Said Yes!

The subconscious mind is set up to protect you when you feel threatened. My husband told me I would have been a hell of a boxer, because I have a fighting subconscious state of mind. I always have my defenses up. Nothing could penetrate my soul because I had built this armor that had protected me for many years. I could never, for the life of me, understand why I had always been so defensive. What I came to realize was that the feeling of not being enough had become my core existence, so I constantly felt the need to fight to represent myself in a positive light. In any situation that seemed to indicate that I was not enough, or had not done enough, I became hyper-defensive.

So, when I walked into my mental courtroom with this mess that was me, I walked in having assumed a dual role: I was both my prosecuting attorney *and* my defense attorney.

Here's the setting: The prosecutor is the accuser of my *lower* self, the version of me that is always up to something, the self that everyone has come to know and expects to show up every time.

The prosecutor is a slick, shrewd character indeed. She is always trying to get me to *accept* that lower version of myself. The defense attorney that lives within is constantly battling to protect and speak to my *higher* self. My defense attorney has always been there and has always wanted to defend me ... but for far too long, I allowed my lower self to believe the lies, as told by me. The defense attorney continues to try to plead her case, which is reflected in my constant attempts to prove myself.

The prosecutor's job is to prove justice. The defense attorney's job is to find the truth, not to convict. Prosecutors are not concerned about right or wrong. But when the defense attorney shows up and delivers the truth, the prosecuting attorney must concede, regardless of what she thinks or what she may say in that final argument. She must submit to the truth.

As a hyper-defensive woman, I would find myself, at every turn, battling with this person and that person. Never could I speak with my voice of reason. *That* voice stayed silent. Every time I tried to speak the truth and tell the world the real scoop, I would get struck down. The prosecutor would get in my ear and start in on me: *Baby Gurl! Baby Guuuurl! Didn't I tell you that you are not worthy? Since you're not worthy, you need to do what the "po-po" [police] say you have the right to do when they arrest you ... remain silent.* The voice would continue: *You just need to accept the fact that you are not, nor have you ever been, anything more than a pawn — a piece, if you will.* I walked around for years believing this lie.

I was not sure what I was going to do to prepare myself for court, or how I was going to do it ... truth be told, I'd begun to believe the prosecutor, and was getting close to admitting defeat. I knew I had to pull it together, take my behind in that courtroom, and strike down the jurors, one by one. Here's how it sent ...

I walk into that Courtroom of Life and take my seat. I am wearing a V-neck sheath dress with three-quarter-length sleeves. The dress is color-blocked, with an asymmetrical red bodice and gray skirt. My haircut is fierce. I must speak my case; I have been called upon by GOD to present it to the world.

The prosecutor has had me imprisoned within myself for years, presenting evidence that was demeaning and not who GOD created me to be. The prosecutor had provided me with false evidence and I'd bought into it. No judge or jury... just me. I'd believed the spoon-fed lies that I was operating in a lower self and had a lower purpose, which was to be pimped out and serve others. There was no real value in who I was as a person and as a woman, I'd been told. And I'd bought into the false prophecy and doctrine of Christel West. I'd bought into the utter chaos and chitter-chatter from church, from family. This resulted in the drowning of the truth of who I was — correction, who I *am*.

But there was something in me that had kept tugging at me, telling me *Christel, this isn't right; this is not who you truly are.*

You have to fix this. So finally, I'd begun doing some research. I had come to realize that I needed to get myself a strong defense, so I'd hired my right-side defense attorney. I had to show the prosecutor where she erred with her false claims as to who I was … the counterfeit me that was constantly put down by everyone.

The prosecutor was trying to accuse me of being myself. I had to *prove* myself to myself. Now I stand before the jury and I must face every fear and every lie the prosecutor has told me in order to be liberated; in order to be free. To free myself, I must take the stand and shut it down. I am so tired of my prosecuting self, bearing all these lies.

Here I stand in the courtroom. It is on now. I am about to show them all who Christel Morgan West is. No more lies, no more fears, no more shame, no more guilt. *You can no longer define what you have no proof to show the world*, I'd show that prosecutor. *I am stronger than you think.*

The prosecutor — the one who'd told me I was naked and made me feel ashamed — had years of evidence, which was reflected in the years of struggle in my life. She told me there were no treasures within me. Although the defense attorney knew better, she'd been challenged to the point of wanting to concede defeat. But something told me to hold on. *Your day in court is coming, and you can finally stand before all who told you that you were no good. You will face your accusers one by one as they surface from that dark panel.*

Only the Judge knows who these accusers were. He always knew. He just wanted me to know what He knew. Now it is time to uncover all the evidence and reveal the treasure. It's always been there. I was just never able to see it.

I now stand here with stacks of briefs — compelling evidence that has been introduced. This is my moment of victory. I will now be vindicated. I had many years to put this together. I'd had no one to do this for me. I had to do this on my own.

***

In my literal case, where I'd been accused to identity theft, we've come to the final day in court. I'd started preparing to go forth as my True Self and empower other women. That afternoon, however, my best friend and I were in a bad accident that left me with a broken knee. And I'm now forced to postpone the conclusion of my trial until I'm able to walk again. I was so close to proving my case. So close.

In just seconds, my life — the life I knew as a mother, wife, entrepreneur, friend, coach, sister, daughter — has been stripped from me via this accident. I have been forced to lie down, something I do not normally do. I knew how to figure out a way to fix a problem; it's what I'd always done. But not this time. I can't fix it. That has led me into a very dark place, a place where I want to give up, give in, lie down and die. Of course, the prosecutor within has begun talking again: You're not good enough … your story will never be told … no one wants to hear what you have to say. *I felt hopeless, useless.*

The truth was that I felt that I was not in control.

Now I am home, post-surgery, with orders not to put any weight on my knee for two months. What? Two whole months? I've taken that to mean I couldn't do anything. The truth is I can't do what I want to do, how I want to do it …which, for me, is a very challenging situation to be in. For a couple of weeks, I refuse to acknowledge that this is my reality. My resistance creates another issue … inner turmoil that has me feeling as though I am going crazy at times. I sleep and sleep. I feel limited — there is so much I could be doing! — and act like I'm completely handicapped. My mother, who's in Detroit at this time, calls me from there every morning to pray with me. I simply hold the phone, responding only with a sarcastic "thank you" as I pretend to be in agreement.

When I finally accept the fact that I can't do things the way I want, I am able to see that there are things I can *do. Resisting gave me tunnel vision; I couldn't see past my circumstance. But when I accept those circumstances, I can see and hear clearly. What I hear is that so many of us allow our circumstances to stop us from doing what we can. It is untrue that I can do nothing. There is a lot I can do; I just have to get out of my own way.*

I realize that GOD has placed me on bed rest to finally deliver this story, this book, this baby, that He had told me to produce for the world to see. He knew I would keep making fear-fueled excuses for procrastinating. And He isn't about to let me do so with any pretenses. My message is solid, and I know my story will resonate with many ... but GOD doesn't want me standing before His people as a counterfeit. When you're born again, something different should exist. GOD is telling me, "You're a counterfeit, Christel. You aren't who I predestined and preordained you to be while you were in your mother's womb. Notice I didn't say 'look like,' because lookalikes abound. Life experiences give birth to the person. You keep trying to protect yourself, wanting to be in control. I wrote your story, remember. As a matter of fact, I wrote the ending in the beginning, so you're just living out the playback."

Amen! My knee healed and, as I mentioned before, my literal court case ended with my being found innocent.

***

My question to you is: What are you resisting? What could you be doing instead of doing nothing?

When you're physically pregnant, the closer you get to giving birth, the more pressure you feel. When you're spiritually pregnant, you're being stretched to give existence to the real you. Head and heart are being placed in proper alignment.

Giving physical birth sometimes involves the use of epidurals, which were created to numb the mother from the waist down to prevent her from feeling. In dealing with my emotional pain, I'd sought a figurative epidural. Because it hurt to feel, I disconnected from my emotions and began numbing myself with relationships, religion, alcohol, food. The problem is that we move forward in life by using our bodies from the waist down. If I kept numbing myself, I would be asleep —existing only, not knowing where I was or what I was doing (denial). And even a literal epidural wears off; at some point the feeling comes back. You can then can choose to push past the pain or ask to be made numb again. And look at what happens when you take antibiotics to clear up an infection. After your body gets used to the antibiotics, they no longer work. Life is the same way. You can only avoid the pain so long; eventually you are going to face the pain again. In facing it, you must make a choice: feel it or numb yourself again, sleep-existing only. Your story will not continue until you *push past the pain!* It's a test that you are going to repeat until you get it.

I had to quit lying to myself and tell the truth, not for anyone else but for me. My perceptions of my experiences were right to me at the time, because that's what I told myself. Telling the truth gave me the boldness to stand in the fire, knowing I would not be burned. So, one day, I decided to get dressed up, go into the delivery room of life, ascend out of my body, assess the old me, and coach her to push out the new me. In the process, I started calling plays, as in football. Yes, I called a huddle between heaven and earth. I started to decree that *this* time, I would not abort; that through me and my testimony, heaven would invade earth. "A leader is coming forth," I decreed, "and she's coming head first! She's blessed coming and going. Why? Because her gift has made room for her. Like JESUS, she binds the brokenhearted and sets the captives free. Like JESUS, she was anointed to deliver others as the Word became flesh. GOD told her that He would make her name great, not for her sake but His. When she was born by the bondwoman, she was naked. Now, she's a free woman ... still naked, but not ashamed!"

Knowing the purpose behind my ordeal prepared me to face my accuser — the enemy within me — in the court of my mind. The generations before me had come to the place I was in; because of the pressure and the intensity involved in birthing something different, they had quit. My purpose was to break the curse and create generational blessings. Because I now knew who I was and what my purpose was, I could stand before my accusers and the prosecutor, convince the jury that I was not a perpetrator of identity theft but rather a victim, and show evidence to prove my innocence.

Rebirth requires you to learn everything all over again. You must become deprogrammed from the old and be reprogramed with the new. Accepting new downloads is easy. The application is difficult, but not impossible.

Iyanla Vanzant discusses this in her book *Get Over It! Thought Therapy for Healing the Hard Stuff*:

The bad programming (virus/thinking) is always trying to filter its way back into our new downloads. It's a strong energy from our subconscious to create what's familiar. Be intentional with positive affirmations throughout the day. If we entertain any negative energy, our subconscious picks it up and plays out what's familiar. We must keep feeding the new systems we're running with positivity, and pay attention to our triggers that will try to cause us to operate in what we've been delivered from.

It's a constant fight to be the true you, because the old you has been in operation for so long. Familiar emotions send messages to our subconscious, and our subconscious picks it up and plays it out! The mind is so powerful.

One thing that helped me was my realization that the mind and brain are separate. The brain can't function unless I give it instructions with my mind. I knew I could change my life with my thinking, but looking at the functions of the brain and the mind was, for me, a revelation. Your thoughts must stay positive.

With any operating system comes the necessity to learn how it works ... and learning involves practicing. We will have system failures, of course, but once we master the use of the system, we will operate a lot easier. Patience is key and paying attention is a must.

Those around us will either empower us or attempt to take our power. The only way our power can be taken is if we allow it. It's important to know the difference between empowerers and power-robbers; we must stay alert. When we were asleep, we just followed. Now, we must lead. In order to do so, we must stay conscious of our thoughts, feelings, emotions and actions so that we can continue feeding the new system and starving the old.

Try creating your own system checklist. Here is mine:

- Did I pray and meditate?
- What am I giving energy to?
- Where are my thoughts?
- What's my why?
- Am I focused, or distracted?
- Are my words, thoughts, and actions positive and uplifting?
- Am I being productive?
- Am I living in the present?
- Am I operating in resistance, or acceptance?
- Have I given my power away?

I'd once said yes to all the lies the prosecutor had on me. I'd accepted these lies every time I'd gone into the courtroom … lies, along with guilt and shame: *I'm not good enough. I'm just another teen statistic.* But not anymore. I made up my mind to head into the courtroom and prove that everything I'd been accused of was false.

Uncovering hidden treasure: my court argument

In the court of life, the defense had to prove that the prosecuting attorney had been lying all along. Now the truth would be unveiled. I started to ask questions. Who told you I was naked? I began.

If I'd never begun asking questions, I would never have uncovered the truth. If I'd never begun asking questions, I would still be living in my lower self. If I'd never begun asking questions, I'd still be living in the lies the prosecutor had presented. If I'd never begun asking questions, I could never stand tall and proud. If I'd never begun asking questions, I'd still be that shameful young girl, imprisoned in a years-long battle. If I'd never begun asking questions, I would still be broken. I had to step outside of myself to discover the truth. But with courage, drive and support around me — and, of course, love — I could stand wise and strong.

We all have had peaks and valleys in our lifetime, each with its own global positioning system. As we each walk our separate journeys, we encounter many distinct faces along the way. We know they are not the same, yet when we tap into their spirits, we find there's not that much that's different. We all have a heartbeat and a pulse ... the current of life that flows within. We each are filled with many winding pathways, all of which lead to the vital center that creates the essence of our being. The Universal Energy (GOD) ultimately sets the course. If we follow and remain obedient to Him, our path is filled with abundance.

If you are making your own journey back to You, never, ever let pride get in the way of your asking for help. Make the investment in yourself. Hire a specialist or life coach. Seek a mentor. Talk to someone who can help you see the truth; help you to trust your spirit and hear again for yourself; and help you speak your truth in confidence. Doing this will position you to use your voice from a place of empowerment; to sound the alarm, through your testimony, for others to wake up to the truth. It's all right to ask for HELP!!

I Am Love

As a teen mother, I was talked about.

As a young woman I still was not good enough.

As an adult, I am still talked about.

I told myself

that if these are the people who say they love me

and this is what Love looks like and feel like,

I don't want it.

When Love showed up

through true family and friends,

I did not recognize it.

I had never felt it

and had no idea

What it was supposed to look or feel like.

I kept my walls up,

afraid to let Love in, because

Love, through my life experiences,

was connected to hurt and pain.

But if all I wanted

was to be loved and accepted,

I had to allow Love in.

I wanted Love

to kick down the thick walls

that existed within me,

but Love wouldn't.

Love wanted to be accepted,

but could not recognize

that it was being rejected by me.

Well ... who is Love?

I am Love.

In order to accept the love I longed for,

searched for, and desired,

I had to accept me.

Who are you?

I am Love.

Self-love and self-acceptance were my twins and the original seeds from which I was created. And in order to find me, I had to say yes to being uncomfortable. I had to say yes to walking away from toxic relationships. I had to say yes to me when everyone else said no. I had to say yes to being different. I made vows to love, honor and obey the spirit within me. I sealed the covenant between my head and heart. I utilized all that lay within me to fulfill my purpose and GOD's plan for my life.

I said YES!

A FINAL WORD

I want you, the reader, to walk away with the understanding that nothing just happens. Everything has a purpose. If we aren't intentional about looking for the good — looking for GOD — in unfavorable situations, we will miss the means of escape that has been provided for us. Third John 2 says:" Beloved, I wish above all things that thou mayest prosper and be in health, even as thy soul prospereth" (KJV). This is why we must look at ourselves, seeking within for the answers to move us forward to our destiny. Your story may not be like mine, but we all have a story. The question is, are you living as the person your DNA indicates you are, the person your life experiences created, or your True Self?

My purpose for sharing my story is to be light for those who can't find their way out of the darkness of their issues. I want you to know that we have all struggled with something, and that we can end the struggle by changing roles in our movies. We are not victims; we are victorious. Our stories have already been written; we must simply trust the process. For us to change roles, our perception must change. Life didn't happen *to* you. It happened *for* you. This is how I had to begin to look at the traumatic experiences that caused me to be stuck for so many years.

I remember talking to a friend who grew up in a two-parent home. Ostensibly, this friend was part of a perfect, functional, nuclear family. But what she didn't realize was that she still had several voids that existed within her. Her mother expected her to be "hang-up-free" … in other words, perfect. Guess how that has played out throughout my friend's life? She overworks herself, and if she doesn't get something right, she beats herself up. Her dad was a great provider; however, he was never present to show her how she should demand that a man treat her. Of course, that brought negative results for her when it came to romance. For some time, my friend denied that her issues stemmed from her childhood. But after looking at her life and the cycle she was repeating, we were able to identify that this 40-plus-year-old woman had experienced a different form of arrested development. She needed to change her perception, forged in her childhood experiences, so that she could take control of her life and live as she desired to live.

When we hold onto a belief system that no longer serves us, it causes us to suffer. The suffering is self-inflicted. You don't have to suffer another day. What you believe about what happened may be true, but it's not the truth of who you are. You are enough. You can be, and do, whatever your heart desires. There is power in choosing you. The power you once unconsciously gave away, you'll consciously take back.

Remember … our thoughts create our feelings, those feelings create our beliefs, and that's why we act the way we act. I allowed my emotions to lead me into a lot of situations because of wrong programming. If you are going to transform your life, you must change your programming. So wipe your hard drive clean. Trust in GOD. Take note of the new mental downloads that will come after you tell yourself, "I will *think* before I *feel*, *believe* and *act*." You won't go wrong!

BIBLIOGRAPHY

Broucaret, F. (2015, July 14). Self esteem: Why do I look at myself in the mirror all the time?

Retrieved from http://www.mariefranceasia.com/lifelove/ decoding/pourquoi-ce-que-je- regarde-le-temps-dans-le-miroir-37569.html

Intimacy. (n.d.). Retrieved from http://www.dictionary.com/ browse/intimacy

Mother-Son Relationship Important for Emotional Growth. (2015, October 06). Retrieved from https://psychcentral.com/ news/2010/03/26/mother-son-relationship-important-for-emotional-growth/12408.html

Premier Abandonment & Attachment-Related Trauma Treatment Center | The Refuge. (n.d.).

Retrieved from http://www.therefuge-ahealingplace.com/ptsd-treatment/abandonment/

Uncover. (n.d.). Retrieved from https://www.merriam-webster. com/dictionary/uncover

Vanzant, Iyanla. (2018) *Get over it! Thought therapy for healing the hard stuff.* Carlsbad, Calif.: Hay House.

About Christel West

C hristel West is a United States based Motivational Speaker and Life Coach. She provides services that include, but not limited to Branding Consultancy, Marketing Strategy, Logo and Graphic Design, Videography and Photography. She recently became an author with her debut, *The Journey Back To Me* a.k.a. *Uncovering The Treasure Within* — a **book** in which she shares her personal **journey** through faith and courage, which has led her to discovering triumph and truth — back to herself.

As a young teenager and single mother, Christel West looked for love in all the wrong places. She lost her identity and covered up about it because of fear and shame. When she realized that she was piling the pain by covering up, she made the decision to be transparent and not ashamed. The **journey** back to find herself has taught her that freedom is a choice and making the choice to be free, led her to want to assist everyone connected to her, to be free as well; thus the inspiration behind authoring the **book**.

Media Contact
Company Name: Book: THE JOURNEY BACK TO ME – Uncovering the Treasure Within
Contact Person: Christel West, Author
Email: Send Email
Country: United States
Website: https://www.christelwest.com/

Made in the USA
Monee, IL
04 February 2023